Le cœur a ses raisons que la raison ne connaît pas.
— Blaise Pascal, *Pensées*

The Poem Has Reasons: A Story of Far Love

SARAH WHITE

DOS MADRES
2022

DOS MADRES PRESS INC.
P.O. Box 294, Loveland, Ohio 45140
www.dosmadres.com   editor@dosmadres.com

Dos Madres is dedicated to the belief that the small press is essential to the vitality of contemporary literature as a carrier of the new voice, as well as the older, sometimes forgotten voices of the past. And in an ever more virtual world, to the creation of fine books pleasing to the eye and hand.

Dos Madres is named in honor of Vera Murphy and Libbie Hughes, the "Dos Madres" whose contributions have made this press possible.

Dos Madres Press, Inc. is an Ohio Not For Profit Corporation and a 501 (c) (3) qualified public charity. Contributions are tax deductible.

Executive Editor: Robert J. Murphy

Illustration & Book Design: Elizabeth H. Murphy
www.illusionstudios.net

The painting on page 47 is a detail from a 1910 portrait of Sarah's mother and mother's mother by Charles Henri Willems. All of the other paintings in this book are by the author, Sarah White.

Typeset in Adobe Garamond Pro & Book Antiqua & Aquiline
ISBN 978-1-953252-53-1
Library of Congress Control Number: 2022933381

First Edition
Copyright 2022 Sarah White
All rights reserved. No part of this book may be reproduced or transmitted in any form or by any means graphic, electronic or mechanical, including photocopying, recording, taping or by any information storage or retrieval system, without the permission in writing from the publisher.
Published by Dos Madres Press, Inc.

ACKNOWLEDGMENTS

I am grateful to editors who have published sections of this memoir.

M. Mark and Enrique Fernandez, for "Six Words and Several Flowers," in the *Village Voice*.

Ricardo Nirenberg and Isabel Nirenberg for "How I Never Learned to Long," in the *Offcourse Literary Journal*.

Michael Schmidt for "The Paper Creature" and "The Little Trobairitz," in *PNR* (*Poetry Nation Review*).

John Murphy for "Bullet Couplets," in the *Lake*.

Christina Thompson for "The Sea Bird," in the *Harvard Review*.

Richard Howard for "Sixteen Sestinas," in the *Western Humanities Review*.

To my mother,
Martha Melhado,
who gave me her memories to put in a book.
I hope this is the one she wanted.
It is dedicated to her.

TABLE OF CONTENTS

PREFACE ~ ix

LIVES & REASONS ~ 1

MY MOTHER'S COMET ~ 43

PATHS TO OC ~ 67

INFERNAL CHAPTERS ~ 95

WOMEN TROUBADOURS ~ 113

THE BRIDGE OF SPIDERS ~ 129

About the Author ~ 155

PREFACE

August 2021

It was in 2006 at the MacDowell Colony that I began writing this book. Granted four weeks there, I devoted most of that privileged time to poring over Dante's *Vita Nuova* (in English translation), concluding that the book I wanted to write on "far love" in my own life was the same book as the one I wanted to write on *amor de lonh* in Troubadour song. I decided to frame that book as a *razo*, borrowed from the same twelfth- and thirteenth-century context: the *razo*, or "Reason," is a short prose story—cogent though probably not "true"—telling how and why a given poem came to be written, something like the "frame" story of the *Arabian Nights* or the *Decameron*. The *Vita Nuova* is an extended *razo* explaining the Reason why Dante wrote his early love poems and, eventually, the *Divine Comedy* itself. Dante's reader is not obliged to accept his explanation at face value, only to recognize the form the poet has given it: he affirms that his story and the poems it contains have a Reason, and that the Reason is a Story of his Distant Love for an ideal young woman named Beatrice. The idea of "Reason" gave my lyric essay one further literary sponsor in Pascal, whose famous maxim *Le Cœur a ses Raisons que la Raison ne connaît pas* places Reason firmly in the human Heart side by side with Memory, Love, and other unknowable human faculties.

Walking in the chill New Hampshire woods, I spotted a mushroom with an intriguing pattern of deeply grooved gills. I picked it and brought it back to my woodland studio, where I dipped it in blue-black ink and laid it on a sheet of plain typing paper to make a primitive monoprint. The resulting figures reminded me of angels, which I appointed as guardians of my project. I knew I would need them, because I sensed in myself a burden of pessimism and self-consciousness likely to prevent me from finalizing the work and pursuing its publication. I am grateful to readers whose interest persuades me now to revise these pages. Those helpers, my *Anges-Champignons*, include Joyce Brown, Eugene Garber, Karen Garthe, David Kramer, Joel Markowitz, France Mugler, Ricardo Nirenberg, Bill Rector, Joel Solonche, and Robert Wexelblatt.

I
LIVES AND REASONS

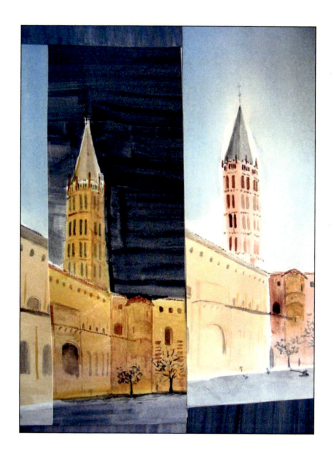

Amor de Lonh - Far Love

Lanquan li jorn son lonc en mai ...
When the days are long in May,
bird song from a far place
enchants me. I am here
recalling a far love,
bowing in such sad thought
that any song or hawthorn flower
might be frozen winter.[1]

Jaufre Rudel of Blaye composed this song about a far love—his greatest joy and sorrow, his sole reason for singing. The first listeners to Jaufre's song wondered who the distant love might be. They enjoyed the idea that it might not be a living woman at all, but the Virgin Mary, or even God. But later listeners didn't enjoy wondering, so after Jaufre's death they composed his Life (*Vida*): the woman he loved was the Countess of Tripoli, a distant city in the Levant whose rulers were Christian (it wouldn't do for a French knight's Lady to be pagan). The anonymous story tells how the troubadour, who had often heard that the Countess was beautiful and full of qualities, decided not just to sing about her, but to enlist in a Crusade and board a ship bound for her Near Eastern home.

... Oh to be a pilgrim
with staff and satchel,
seen by her lovely eyes.

---

[1] All the translations in this book, unless otherwise noted, are mine.

On the ship, he became ill and arrived in Tripoli dying. Messengers rushed to tell the Countess, who, taking up her role in the story, rushed to the crusader's side. Jaufre was unconscious. She embraced him. He woke, knowing that this embrace had fulfilled his deepest longings and that he could not survive it. He died in the Countess's arms and was buried in great pomp. His Lady entered a convent, where she devoted the rest of her life and thought to a knight she had only seen once and a God she had never seen at all.

Map of France I

The town of Blaye lies in Haute Gironde, "historic boundary between the language of *Oïl* in the North and *Oc* in the South." According to the *Blue Guide to Southwest France* (2003), its attractions include the ruined château of Jaufre Rudel, "author of *Amours lointains* [who] left for Tripoli in 1147 in pursuit of his beloved Melissande, only to expire in her arms."

There is no *Amours lointains* written by Jaufre or by anyone else. Knowingly or not, the guidebook's writer has transmitted a fiction invented seven hundred years ago in Jaufre's *vida* and adapted in Edmond Rostand's nineteenth-century play *La Princesse Lointaine*.

I have visited a number of places described in the *Blue Guide*, but not Blaye. I haven't felt the need to visit Jaufre's traces. Instead, I have chosen to admire him *de lonh*, from afar, at several removes from the legend. Like the *vida* author, I have made his poems and those of others including myself into stories of how the poems came to be written. I will tell how, when a near love of mine became a far one, he left me with poems. I will tell how my earliest far love drew me to southwest France, to Occitan troubadours, and to Dante.

A Note on Occitan

Today, the *Blue Guide*'s "boundary between the language of *Oïl* in the North and *Oc* in the South" is invisible and inaudible. Nowhere in North or South are travelers likely to hear the language of *Oc* unless they seek it out. Since the time of King Francis and his 1539 edict, the language of *Oui* (successor to *Oïl*) has been France's sole official language. But when the troubadours flourished, in the twelfth and thirteenth centuries, France was a kingdom of loosely knit regions whose princes were often more powerful than the King. Vernacular speech in some of those regions was quite distinct from that of the King's subjects in Île de France. People of Poitiers, for example, did not speak like people of Troyes. Their songs differed as much as lark songs from thrush songs, which is why the first troubadour, Duke Guilhem IX of Poitiers, wrote that the birds were singing *chascus en lor lati,* each in his distinct Latin dialect, though of course they were all singing of love.

Until recently, the troubadours' language and its modern descendant were generally referred to as Provençal, but Provence is only one region in Occitania, and Provençal only one of its main dialects (the others are Gascon, Limousin, and Languedocien). Those who speak, sing, write, and advocate the language tend to call it Occitan, and that is what I shall call it in this book.

Here is another story of how a poem came to be written in Occitania.

Reasons for Reasons

Years ago, when I was writing poems even more rarely than I write them today, I decided to try a sestina. I had not read very many and had no particular theme in mind.

My only goal was to follow the rules for end-words in their required spiral order. The result didn't please me, and I put it away. Later, when I found it, I had to try to imagine the person who might have produced such a strange poem, and I wrote this story about him:

....

Six Words and Several Flowers

Of the works of the troubadour Gaucelm Laudet only two have come down to us: a sestina and the fragment of a love canso.

It is said that the first object of Gaucelm's love was Lady N and that this noblewoman's virtues were tarnished by False Pride, which made her cold to his affection. She never answered his messages or songs. She averted her eyes when he came into the room. Venting his despair, he wrote:

> Winds from strange places
> fetch day's rain.
> Black flints
> make the rock
> smart.

He never finished the canso. Before he'd written its closing lines, he glimpsed one of N's companions, Lady L, and guessed from her smiling appearance that she would not refuse him. In fact, Poet and Lady took up an exchange of messages and songs that delighted them both.

Meanwhile, the opening of the canso was seen by a painter who slept in Gaucelm's rooms on nights when he found them unoccupied. Admiring the achingly opaque verses, he decided to illustrate them in a drawing.

He drew a grey star. At its center, a black line merged into lighter shades near the edges. From two points, angling in opposed diagonals toward the lower corners, he drew broken lines resembling rain, each "drop" shaped like entwined initials: G.N.

The broken lines fell toward a lower, flower-like figure, as if to straddle or inscribe it between two compass points. This figure, like the star, had a shaded center and light sides, but was more like a starfish than a star, the outlines curved instead of angular. In spaces to the right and left, wavy lines in shades of blue suggested the east and west coastlines of some long continent, or the embodiments of winds.

The artist finished his drawing, but as it was useless to him, the illustration of an incomplete poem, he left it in Gaucelm's room. Later, word came that the Count of

Limoges needed artisans to decorate a chapel. In quest of this or some other commission, the painter quitted Gaucelm's region, never to return.

It happened that Gaucelm had an irritable landlord,

Truc the apothecary. Prowling one day in the poet's empty rooms, he came across the drawing and the lines that had inspired it. Thinking image and poem were by the same person, he deduced that Gaucelm must be ill from deflected black bile. The truth was that at the very moment when he drew this grim conclusion, Gaucelm and Lady L were amusing themselves in a field of lavender.

The druggist knew a local Abbot who sought some excuse to silence Gaucelm. Chivalric families, protectors of the Abbey, claimed his songs provoked irreverence and rebellion in their adolescent children. The druggist conveyed his diagnosis to the Abbot, who appointed Truc as medical officer in the Abbey. They agreed that the troubadour should be placed under official supervision.

One afternoon, as Gaucelm lay with Lady L on the fragrant hillside, armed knights seized him, carried him to the Abbey, and locked him in a cell—an unlit, stifling place reserved for those guilty of Accidia and Despair.

In a matter of days, the diet of undressed cabbage leaves, the droning of the monks' prayers, and the absence of his lady had so unhinged the poet that he lapsed into genuine despair, then into a restless, wordless trance. His poetic gifts were active only when he slept, and as good as lost to the world.

He remained in this despondency for over a year. The high-handed Abbot died and was replaced, but his successor never asked why Gaucelm had been confined to the dark cell. He just supposed the somnolent poet incapable of living outside it.

Two years after Gaucelm's arrest, Francis of Assisi, on a pilgrimage, chose the Abbey as a stopping place. Hearing there was a poet confined in the cloister, he asked permission to see him. A moment with Gaucelm suggested to Francis that the poet's muteness might be curable, though the treatment would have to be subtler than that of an ordinary melancholic. How could he coax song from the incoherent world of dream?

Francis, a poet himself, specialized in sacred cansos but also knew the secular forms, one of which he used for Gaucelm's therapy. He asked the poet to sit beside him near a well in the cloister garden and asked him if he knew the pattern of a sestina. Even half-awake, the patient recalled "The firm desire that enters …," by a troubadour who, though dead for half a century, was still known throughout Occitania. Gaucelm named the six end-words of Arnaut Daniel's sestina: Enter, Fingernail, Soul, Rod, Uncle, Chamber.

"If you composed a sestina," asked Francis, "what would your end-words be?"

Gaucelm shut his eyes as if to consult figures on the linings of his eyelids.

> "*Spider* would be one."
> "and …"
> "*Vessel.*"
> "Good. Now four more."

> "*Fathom. Cousin. Answer.* I can't find …"
> "Try," said the pilgrim.
> "*Ravel,*" said the poet.

The sestina has a spiral form. Its lines do not rhyme, but they derive coherence from a revolving order of the end-words and from minute progressions in their meaning. Francis, hoping to startle art from sleep, told Gaucelm to concentrate on the words, letting them turn until they fell into sequence.

Near the well, thyme-flowers gave off spicy perfume. A swarm of bees was gathering nectar, and the sick poet stayed transfixed for hours. He saw bees turning in the air as the line-ends turned in his ear and brain. The six words lengthened and contracted, becoming negative, positive, verbal, nominal, singular and plural. There was little stress in the work, only a slight acceleration of the pulse, monitored by Francis, Gaucelm's physician and friend. By the time the poem was finished, its composer had found the strength to sing "Ravel and Unravel":

> Deep in the folds of sleep, a vessel
> holds a soul, a sort of cousin,
> hidden, hoping never to be fathomed.
> He swims like the whiskers of a spider.
> First words, then other words, he ravels
> while I wait, intent, and want an answer.
>
> I, because I weep for an answer,

he, because he travels in vessels,
wander in the kingdom of these ravels.
No one, not a sister, not a cousin,
measures. He is slighter than a spider
and dark as seven hundred fathoms.

Should he ever stir, rise, fathom
my intent, strange would his answer
be, not plain. Any spider
draws secret patterns on the vessel
where no witless cook or cousin
will unbend the ravels

and fantasies. The soul no sooner ravels
them than wraps them in fathoms
for the father of another cousin
to decipher, sifting till an answer
splits. Can a steward on the vessel
read language rendered from a spider?

Do not seek to ramify the spider
nor ask what is netted and raveled
in the sheet. (Veering with the vessel,
a bug is balancing between the fathom
and the plant.) Someone turns to answer
in the words of a watchman to his cousin.

Once, an unknown uncle of my cousin
wrote a Treatise on the Latin Spider
yet failed to frame an answer.
Ravel means to ravel and unravel.
The pain is delicate to fathom

    on a trip more rapid than the vessel.

    Song, you sang no answer. What's a spider?
    Who ravels? Only tell my cousin
    where to seek our vessel in the fathoms.

Listeners agreed that the sestina made no sense,
but that its sonorities showed high poetic ambition
belying suspicions of Gaucelm's Accidia. Francis
suggested that the poet be allowed to leave the
Abbey for a court where an audience might
appreciate his talents. On his release, Gaucelm
sought the estate where Lady L was mistress.
She took him in. His spirits revived. He sent her
countless cansos; she replied with witty messages.
Occasionally, they escaped to a lavender hillside.

After ten contented years, the lady died giving
birth to twin daughters, the poet's own. The infants
were adopted by a wealthy lord, L's widower, and
Gaucelm traveled to Umbria to look for Francis.
By then, the Saint, too, had died after founding a
community of brothers, who welcomed the poet
with open arms.

They gave Gaucelm a plot of thyme and an acre
of lavender. For the remainder of his days, he sang
and gardened, gardened and sang. It is said that in
hundreds of songs, now lost, he praised the flowery
nectars and the scent of his lady's flesh, perfumes he
hoped to breathe one day in Paradise.

    ....

Other Reasons

The poem "Ravel and Unravel," when I found it in the drawer half-forgotten like the mad, mute troubadour, looked strange enough to have been written by someone else. I imagined Gaucelm, then Lady N, Lady L, Truc, and the Abbot. Saint Francis wandered in. Through an unlikely chain of events, the story I wrote appeared in the *Village Voice*, which didn't normally publish fiction. The *Voice*'s literary editor got an indignant letter from one reader saying there had never been a troubadour named Gaucelm Laudet and that "Ravel and Unravel" could not be a thirteenth-century poem. The indignant letter was right on both counts.

The prose in "Six Words and Several Flowers" constitutes what was called, in Old Occitan, a *razo* (reason) purporting to explain the genesis of a given poem. In a number of manuscripts, the *razo* was juxtaposed to the *vida*, a fictional biography. The story of Jaufre Rudel and the Countess of Tripoli is a *vida* containing elements of *razo* about the genesis of the mysterious song, *Lanquan li jorn*.

"Six Words and Several Flowers," a *razo* explaining my poem "Ravel and Unravel," could be followed by another *razo* explaining "Six Words," beginning an infinite regression. Though I wrote the tale decades ago, and don't know exactly why I did, that would not have stopped a medieval *razo* writer. Consider the following *razo*, inserted in a *vida* of Bernard de Ventadour. Bernard is perhaps the most admired of all troubadours, and "When I see the lark" his most admired song. Its melody invites the listener to imagine the ascension and fall of an ecstatic lark:

> When I see the lark
> joyfully move its wings toward the sun
> Until it forgets and lets itself fall
> as sweetness takes hold of its heart,
> Alas! how envious I am
> of any joyful man I see!
> It's a wonder my heart
> doesn't melt with desire.
>
> Alas, I thought I knew so much
> about love …

This is how the *razo* writer, who may or may not have heard the music, claims to explain the lark poem. He says the great troubadour frequented the Duchess of Normandy's court, loved her, and sang many songs for her: Bernard called her "Lark" because of a knight who loved her and whom she called Ray [*Rai*, sunlight]. And one day, the knight came to the Duchess's room. The lady, seeing him, raised the hem of her cloak and put it on his neck, and let herself fall on the bed. And Bernard saw it all because one of the Countess's servants had let him watch secretly. And he wrote a song about it:

> When I see the lark …

As this example shows, *razos* can be preposterous. Who would take this farcical account to explain Bernard's song of ecstatic love? There can be no authoritative *razo*. The poem has reasons that Reason doesn't know. But a *razo* may be a good story and keep the poem company as it goes in search of an audience.

The Razo Game

In the year 1275, a middling Man of Letters makes his penurious way across Northern Italy, to Padua, say, where a Lord and Lady have commissioned him to compile a *chansonnier* (poetry anthology) for their library. In his luggage are several Occitan manuscripts, and in one of these he finds the following *tenso,* or debate poem, between a certain Bernard Arnaut and an otherwise unknown *trobairitz* (woman troubadour). He doesn't know much about the two poets, who have been dead for fifty years or so, but he chooses the *tenso* because the woman's name, Lombarda, and some place names mentioned in the exchange might interest his Italian hosts. Here is the *tenso* translated into English by Bruckner, Shepard, and White in *Songs of the Women Troubadours*:[2]

> Bernard Arnaut:
>
> I'd like to be a Lombard for Lady Lombarda;
> I'm not as pleased by Alamanda or Giscarda.
> She looks at me so kindly with her sweet eyes
> that she seems to love me, but too slowly,
> for she withholds from me sweet sight
> and pleasure
> and keeps her lovely smile
> to herself; no one can move her.
>
> Lord Jordan, if I leave you Allemagna,
> France, Poitou, Normandy and Brittany,
> surely you should leave me, uncontested,
> Lombardy, Livorno and Lomagna.

---

[2] *Songs of the Women Troubadours*, edited and translated by Matilda Bruckner, Laurie Shepard, and Sarah White, with a preface by W. S. Merwin. Garland, 2000.

And if you'll be my ally
I'll be ten times more yours
with your own lady, a stranger
to all baseness.

Mirror of Worth,
comfort is yours.
Let the love in which you bind me
not be broken for a villain's sake.

Lombarda:

I would like to have the name Bernarda,
and to be called, for Lord Arnaut, Arnauda;
and many thanks, my lord, for being so kind
as to mention me alongside two great ladies.
I want you to say
without concealment
which one pleases you the most,
and in which mirror you are gazing.

For mirroring and absence so discord
my inner chords that I can barely stay accorded,
but, remembering what my name records,
my thoughts accord in good accordance.
Still, I wonder
where you've put your heart;
neither its house nor hut
can be seen. You keep it silent.

The Man of Letters thinks this poem will please his hosts, especially if he enhances it with a little story about the debaters.

Who are they? Why, in an apparent love-plea, is Bernard Arnaut so concerned with exchange of territories? Why does Lombarda reject his plea with such sarcasm and anger?

First, Bernard. The Man of Letters recognizes the name as that of several Dukes of Armagnac. He can safely make the troubadour Duke of that Gascon region. But no, it would be better to make him the Duke's younger brother, who still lacks the title, castle, and access to all the brandy he can drink. Such a man was likely to be more covetously scheming than the Duke himself, and looser in his courting habits.

As for Lombarda, she's obviously a poet, skilled in technicalities of rhyming and word-play. She knows how to interweave words of the same family (accord, record, etc.), a practice the Man of Letters admires. Where does she live? Not in Armagnac. Bernard is the kind of man who is inspired by distance from the one desired. Perhaps, like the great Jaufre Rudel, he has fallen in love with a woman without seeing her (*sez la vezer*). But Bernard is no Jaufre, capable of loving a lady as far away as Tripoli. Let's put her in Toulouse, only a day or two on horseback from Armagnac. That way, the distance can be narrowed to create friction between them, then widened again to provoke the Lady's indignation. That's all that's needed by way of a story. And here it is, as it may be found on parchment in Manuscript H, Vatican Library, lat. 3207 (excerpt edited and translated by Bruckner, Shepard, and White):

> Na Lombarda was a lady of Toulouse, gracious, fair, lovely in her person, and learned. She could compose well, and she made beautiful, amorous verses. Don Bernard Arnaut, brother of the Duke of Armagnac, heard of her goodness and merit and came to Toulouse

to see her. He lived in great intimacy with her, sought her love, and was very much her friend. He wrote these verses about her, and sent them to her in her house. Then he mounted his horse, and, without seeing her, went away to his own country.

I'd like to be a Lombard, etc.

Na Lombarda was much amazed when she heard that Lord Bernard Arnaut had left without seeing her, and she sent him these verses:

I would like to have the name Bernarda, etc.

Or the Man of Letters scenario is somewhat different. Let's say he doesn't invent the *razo* himself, but transcribes it from a performance in which he has heard one, two, or three singers play the roles of Lord, Lady, and Narrator, to animate a song composed some years before.

There is an analogy in the modern event called a poetry reading. Here, the poet typically inserts passages of prose between the poems by way explanation, or as a way of inviting listeners' goodwill. Often, the poet adds too much prose, and the audience becomes impatient and suspicious: if the poems require so much commentary, they may not be strong enough to stand on their own. "Stop giving Reasons," we think. "Get on with the Poem." There was a troubadour named Guillem de la Tor. According to his *vida*, "when he wanted to recite his songs he made his discussion of the explanation longer than the song itself." When I read poems in front of an audience, I remember Guillem de la Tor and try to avoid his mistake.

There's also the issue of music. The *tenso*, at first, was probably sung by a man and a woman, or two men with voices in different registers, or even a single versatile performer. Compelling expression and tone would have sufficed to enliven the stanzas. Think of a soprano and baritone performing a duet like Irving Berlin's "Anything You Can Do (I Can Do Better)." We don't need to know the characters' identities or the song's occasion. Some troubadour *chansonniers* include melodies, but many, like the manuscript containing this *tenso*, do not. Perhaps *razos* were written partly to compensate for the absence of music.

Be that as it may, I suggest you take a poem—your own or someone else's—and tell the reason it came to be written. If you don't know the reason, invent one. Or invent the story first and then the poem it pretends to explain. All these are good variations of the *Razo* Game.

Later, I'll tell you the Sestina Game.

More Reasons

Razos generally involve some love difficulty the poet was having when he or she wrote the poem. In this spirit, I would begin the *razo* for "Six Words" with a love problem I was having at the time I wrote it. But I forget who I was in love with in 1980. That's not quite true. I remember a name. I just don't remember the pain. After labor, a woman remembers writhing, and screaming for anesthesia, but has no direct access, thank goodness, to the agony she felt while writhing and screaming. In order to have a usable sense memory of that love and its sufferings, I'd have to consult a journal I'd written at the time. But I didn't keep a journal of loves, only a journal of dreams. One clue to the reason for "Six Words" is that it came in a period when the hours I spent dreaming were the privileged times of my life. Numb to possibilities of near love or far, I could say of myself what I said of Gaucelm: *His poetic gifts, active only when he slept, were as good as lost to the world.*

I wasn't in prison like him, of course. I was keeping house, teaching students, and earning a salary, but I was cloistered, unhopeful, attending mostly to dreams, and reading Borges. I had discovered *fausse érudition,* the literary genre that playfully falsifies learning for the sake of discovery, not deception. In those days, the woods, especially Argentinian and Italian woods, were full of *fausse éruditon.* That's where I wanted to play and live rather than in Lancaster, Pennsylvania, where I was keeping house, teaching students, and earning a salary. My path to the woods was indirect.

Detour: Farewell to Fabliaux

The following tale was written in Old French, somewhere north of the Oc–Oïl boundary.

Three Ladies Who Found a Phallus

Walking from I don't know where
to Mont Saint Michel, three ladies
found two balls and one fat prick
wrapped in a cloth with just the tip
showing. Lady One noticed, snatched it,
slipped it in her dress, I hear.
Lady Two asked for a share.

"Finders keepers!" said her friend.
"Are you crazy? It's half mine!
Of course I have my rights.

> You know I'm your companion
> on this pilgrimage." "So what?
> I don't care. You'll get neither part
> nor whole!" Lady Two took this to heart.
>
> She swore she'd have it—unless
> some judge should rule against her,
> but who? "Now that you mention it, nearby
> stands a house of nuns and holy women
> praying for the world. We'll ask the Abbess
> her opinion. She'll feel flattered."
> "Oïl! Let's do it," said the other.

Though the title and first line announce three ladies, only two ever speak in the story. My addendum, which is not for scholarly consumption, adds a few lines to account for the presence of a third lady.

> Lady Three was shy and mute.
> She frowned, smiled, shook her head
> and nodded, showing she agreed
> with Ladies One and Two. They went
> along until they found the convent
> governed by an Abbess. When they asked
> for her, they heard she was at Mass.
>
> "We'll wait," the Ladies said,
> and sat down in the audience room.
> Soon, the Abbess, the Prioress,
> and Stewardess arrived. Up rose Lady
> One: "Thank God you've come. My friend
> refuses ..." Lady Two burst in: "... to share
> something she has in her care!"

Then she told how they'd found it,
and how they wanted to submit
their quarrel for the Abbess's decision.
"Well, bring it out where I can have
a look. Then I'll decide." "Yes, dear,
show Her Reverence the prick.
She will make a judgement quick."

Fabliaux are full of the French three-letter words that correspond to English four-letter words. One time, weary of the usual equivalents for *vit, con,* etc., I decided to substitute meaningless monosyllables, and was surprised at how hard it was to find them! I came up with *zikk* for prick, *fonn* for cunt, and *noop* for what the characters do with *zikks* and *fonns*. A lot of nooping goes on in fabliaux, though not in this one. By the way, the original Old French tales are in eight-syllable rhymed couplets. Luckily for you, I'm not adopting that tedious form here, except for a little rhyme at the end of each stanza.

"… She will make a judgement quick."
And the Lady who had found it
drew the prick from her bosom
and placed it before the nuns,
who stared at it fondly. But I swear
it was the abbess who gazed
most eagerly. She sighed three long
drawn-out sighs, and said: "You're wrong!

I won't award to one of you
something that belongs to us!
It's neither yours nor your companions'.
Just the other day, the bolt was stolen

from our convent door, and I demand
it be restored, the abbey's gain.
Then she spoke to Dame Elaine,

standing near the Stewardess. "See
that it's returned to where it came from.
That's my wish." Sister Elaine
took it in her slim, white sleeve.
The ladies, who'd lost out,
departed weeping, never again
to ask the Abbess's opinion!

Next time they found such an object
they'd keep it as a precious relic.

Years ago, I had a chance to become an internationally known specialist in Old French bawdy tales.

I discovered them deep in the stacks of the University of Michigan Library after completing a doctorate in Old French literature. The Arthurian romances and Christian Saints' Lives I'd studied offered ample opportunity for further academic work, but the raunchy fabliaux seemed to offer something else—a bit of fun, which I missed in my life as an underemployed PhD entering her middle years. My future looked brighter on the day I received from *Playboy* a check, adorned with a tiny bunny, in payment for my translation of *La Sorisete aux Estopes,* "The Little Rag Mouse." In that tale, a Peasant marries without ever having had sex with a woman. On the wedding night, his more experienced bride deceives him by claiming to have left her *fonn* at her mother's house in the next town. When the Peasant goes to look for it and bring it home, he leaves space in their bed for her lover, the Priest. And the Mouse? I'll tell you about her later. What matters is that checks from *Playboy* did not arrive frequently, and I had to look for a respectable job. I looked for three years before finding one in the French and Italian Department of Franklin & Marshall, a small Pennsylvania college. In 1982, thanks in part to publishing a lengthy, much-footnoted article on "Sexual Language and Human Conflict in the Old French Fabliau," I earned tenure, and with it, a sabbatical leave. I wondered where I would go—timid traveler that I am.

At professional conferences, I had found that giving papers on three-letter words was a good way to flirt. (I was not too timid for that.) During one meeting of the Northeast Modern Language Association, a Québécois medievalist and former Dominican monk flirted back, and I would eventually pursue him to his northern lair. To the dean of my liberal arts college and the Center for Medieval Studies at the University of Montreal I proposed my project: a monograph "On the Circulation of Animals in Old French Fabliaux." In autumn of 1983, Québec greeted me warmly, charmingly, abundantly. I wrote:

In Montreal, a Professor of French Goes Mad

I am well come to a town
with a Coast of Snows,
a Coast of Saint Catherine, patron
of spinsters and women in labor.
Here is the Avenue of Pines.
Here are the hands,
on Jeanne Mance Street,
of Marjolaine, the masseuse.

I feel her patois
improve me.
Merci, I say …

Then, the winds turned cold, and the first sleet fell on Côtes des Neiges. I had foolishly tried to turn a far love into a near one. I watched my idyll go the way of all idylls, and, without it, found my scholarly task too heavy to bear.

> *Merci,* I say …
> *Bienvenue,*
> she replies: Welcome, and not
> (as they say in Paris)
>
> For nothing …
> There is no for which …
>
> O.K. 'Bye, Marjolaine.
>
> *Bonne fin de semaine!*
> Sings the man in the rain.

Having said good-bye to the man in the rain, I laid aside the monograph forever, and with it the chance of becoming an international specialist in Old French bawdy tales. Then, in order not to go really mad—as mad as Gaucelm Laudet in his prison cell—I needed a new task, one that would work as Gaucelm's sestina had worked for him.

Unwritten Monograph "On the Circulation of Animals in Old French Fabliaux" (outline)

A. Basic Fabliau Joke: Because of a Woman's scheme, a Peasant Husband is cuckolded by Priest, Monk, or Wandering Clerk. The typical fabliau ends when the scheme succeeds, for example, at the moment when the Peasant, thinking his Wife has left her *fonn* at her Mother's, goes to fetch it and the Priest can replace him in bed.

B. Basic Joke Elaborated: "The Little Rag-Mouse" follows the Peasant to his Mother-in-law's house where the reader sees further results of the scheme. When he announces his errand, the older woman registers no surprise at being asked for the *fonn,* but figures her daughter is plotting something interesting and falls in with the plot. She hands her son-in-law a basket of rags. "Here, take this. It's in the basket."

C. Further Elaboration: The Peasant goes off across the field, where he is overcome by a desire to perform, here and now, the act he has heard so much about (a novel variation on far love!) He unbuttons his fly. Unbeknownst to anyone, a Mouse has made its nest in the rags. Frightened by the *zikk* that looms before it, the Mouse jumps from the basket and scampers away, stopping some distance off to taunt the Peasant with high-pitched squeaks. The panicked bridegroom gives chase and tries to lure the *fonn* with assurances that he will treat it well and let it go back to bed before forcing himself upon it. No more *nooping* away from home, he promises, but the Mouse will have none of him and disappears.

D. Disheartening Dénouement: The stymied Peasant returns and climbs into bed, where his Wife consoles him: Don't worry. The *fonn* has come home after all. But the bridegroom finds that it's no longer as fresh as it should be, having been soiled "by falling in the dew." At which point the tale-teller adds a moral, though who knows how seriously it is meant to be taken.

> I've taught you by this fable
> That Woman is the Devil.
> Strike out both my eyes
> If this is bad advice.

> She'll hoodwink anyone
> With her brain or tongue.
> Husband, watch your spouse
> Or lose your own Rag Mouse.

My monograph would not concern itself with morals but would focus on the metamorphoses of the Mouse. Where did it go after escaping the Peasant? We know it didn't reenter the household or play a further role in the Wife/Peasant/Priest triangle. This Mouse of Imagination, having shape-shifted into a rag and a runaway vulva, had recently become a check for $400! A month of groceries for me and my kids. I reflected that the anonymous rhymer who first recited "La Sorisete" might also have received grocery-money in exchange for his Joke, Elaborations, Dénouement, and Moral.

That was to be the theme of my monograph: Exchange. Transformation, Money.

The heyday of fabliaux was the thirteenth and fourteenth centuries, which, I had been led to understand, corresponded with the rise of town economies in Northern France, with commercial fairs, merchant guilds, and other ways of getting around taboos on lending and circulating money.

To think I was planning to master all that social history and economic theory, to read the Church fathers and their writings against Usury, to trace the development of coinage and currency, and ... Poor Little Mouse, by the time I was through with her she would have become so laden with false (really false!) erudition, so poisoned with ill-digested jargon, that she could not have scampered across another field or hidden in another rag-basket. I don't regret that monograph. But I miss the Mouse and wonder what became of her.

A Mouse's Crisis

She runs across a wheatfield, refugee
from Paradise in widow's rags—
estopes, stuff, washed and shredded,
shredded and washed
to a tee.
The mouselet has lived a soft life
and never learned ancestral ways
of surviving on grain from husks
fallen in muddy furrows—stale, mildewy
grain, though she would gladly eat some now,
God knows.
The night is cold.
Is there shelter? Here! Stone wall.
A chink. "I'll crawl in." She flops—
Whoops—to the floor of an unlit room.
Someone's kitchen?
What's that smell?

Molten wax, burnt wicks, stale incense
in the anteroom where a Priest
dons his robes, the Priest
we met before,
but he's not here.
He's home asleep, having nooped
the Peasant's Wife. He may or may not
come Sunday to say Mass.
(He seldom does, being lazy

and without true vocation.)
That is why,
in the vestry cupboard, unused
wafers lie—their scent just strong
enough to guide her.
She has found
a crawl hole in the back.
She has found the Host
and more—another mouse.
They share.
And when the Priest
arrives some Sundays hence to check
on his supplies, they're gone, as gone
as Christ's body from its tomb
on Easter morning—
Bread, trans-
substantiated to a trail of oval pellets—
Call them "tell-tale" pellets.
And the Mouse?
she'll leave her hairless
nurselings and move on.

Sixteen Sestinas

The project I dreamed up expressed a poetic *Amor de Lonh*. My near loves were far away—friends and sons. I had two grown sons: Malcolm, a first-year grad student at Columbia, and Owen, a junior at the University of Massachusetts, who told me he'd meant to write me but "hadn't been able to find a Canadian stamp." No one I knew seemed able to find a Canadian stamp. Though this was long before e-mail, letter-writing was becoming obsolete, and I cast about for a way to elicit mail from my far friends.

In downtown Montreal, there were plenty of Canadian stamps, and I sent out the call in the following letter:

> To: selected friends
> Montreal
> Re: a request for words
> October 6, 1983
>
> Lately, I have been making sestinas out of dialogues with friends. In the earliest sestina we know, Arnaut Daniel worked the unlikely and unpoetic words *Oncle* and *Ongla* (Uncle and Nail) into a love poem, a game-like challenge, of course, but a good sestina is more than a game … Two people have already given me their 6 words and were pleased with the results. One says of his sestina:
>
> "I love to read it when I'm stoned, though it sounds nice when I'm not, too."
> Another writes:
> "It is good to give someone 6 words and get back a poem … [it] becomes a conversation between us."
> If enough people would let me have their words, I might eventually put together a collection …
> Petrarch preferred nouns as end-words, but other poets have widened the field. Your words can be of any kind: common or proper nouns, verbs, adverbs, or adjectives. They need not have the same number of syllables or the same "beat." They shouldn't rhyme. Some of the words can be incongruous in the context of the others. I just ask that they be words that please, amuse, interest, or obsess you.

If you will send a beworded note or card, I will send back your sestina as soon as I'm happy with it. Best wishes and thanks.

Sarah

Samples Enclosed

One of the samples was my version of Dante's *al poco giorno e al gran cerchio d'ombra,* his homage to the troubadour Arnaut Daniel.

> To the short days, to the long, circling shadows
> I come, alas, to whitening mountains,
> and to the time when grass
> loses color; but my desire stays green
> implanted as it is in the hard stone
> that speaks and feels as if it were a lady.

Dante would never have solicited end-words from a friend, no more than a master chef would solicit recipes from a rival cook. The great Florentine knew that the words he wanted were *ombra, colle, erba, verde, petra, donna. Shadow* would react ominously with *mountain; stone* would abrade the *green* of *grass,* and the tense relationships would create the image he wanted of a particular *lady.*

> Another simulacrum: This new lady
> stays frozen as the snow in shadow
> as unmoved as any stone
> by the sweet season that warms mountains
> and turns them from white to green
> by scattering flowers and grass.

Rotating incompatibles would carry the poet into a harsh season from which he attempts to escape through memory and wish ...

> When, in her hair, she wears a tress of grass,
> driving from my mind all other ladies,
> a curl of yellow mingles with the green,
> and Love itself rests in that shadow;
> Love holds me in its little mountains
> more firmly than mortar holds a stone.

> ... though most often memory and wish only
> intensify the harshness.

> Her beauty has more power than any stone.
> Its wound cannot be healed by herb or grass.
> I've fled across the plains and mountains
> because I would escape such a lady.
> Against her light no shadow
> falls from hill, wall, or bough of green.

> Once, I saw her dressed in green,
> so lovely she would turn to stone
> the love I feel, even for her shadow.
> I desired her in a field of grass,
> she as amorous as any lady,
> and the field, encircled by high mountains.

By the fifth stanza (if not before!), monotony sets in. But just as we weary of the stony landscape, the poet turns it upside down with a classical "impossibility" figure:

> Yet rivers will flow into the mountains,
> before that timber, soft and green,

> is kindled like a lovely lady
> loving me. And I would sleep on stone
> each night, or graze on grass,
> to see the place her skirt casts shadows.

Standing on its head, the poem takes a fleeting look under the lady's skirt before pulling out over a wintry panorama.

> When mountains cast the deepest shadows,
> a youthful lady covers them with green-
> ness, as men hide stone under the grass.

I've lost the other sample I included with my call for words, a sestina of mine. I know Fox, Moon, and Ruby were three of the end-words, and I'm sure the friend for whom I wrote it was kind to say the poem "sounded nice" when he wasn't stoned. I must have reread "Nocturnal Fox" at some point, felt ashamed of it, and thrown it away. Yet that poem was no more embarrassing than the others. They were all beginner poems, especially embarrassing because I wasn't young when I wrote them. As art, the Sestina Game project was doomed for a dozen reasons, but instead of enumerating them, I'm trying to write its *razo*.

Angela

I got several letters. (All my friends love words, and several love games, too.) The response that lingered longest in my mind came from my Italian colleague, Angela Jeannet. It arrived in an envelope which, when opened, released six tiny paper parachutes, each bearing a word: Memory, Morning, Tender, Fire Thorn, Sea, and Quartz. I would labor (all too hard!) to construct *nontiscordardime* (forget-me-not) and to show off my acquaintance with Angela's language.

> Sometimes you need a medieval Art of Memory
> to recall the hours: Morning,
> remembered as a dim and tender
> summons; noon screams like a fire thorn;
> evening spreading on a bay or sea;
> night and virtues, bright as quartz.

That sestina peters out half-way through the second stanza, though there are two nice lines near the end:

> On overleaves, the autumn's tender
> quail dart in and out of memory.

The poem has no life in it. No death either.

Lorenzo

Lorenzo Pezzatini, a Florentine like Angela, is a conceptual artist specializing in string: meters and meters of it, bright yellow with dollops of red and blue acrylic paint squeezed through a pastry tube to look like thorns on a stem. He twists, weaves, drapes, and coils the stuff around indoor and outdoor spaces and sometimes around himself, in configurations requiring great patience on his part. "Have a little pity," he says to his audience, pity for his obsession, for his bewildering project, for his defiance of practicality. His plea resounds in my mind as I contemplate the strings of sestinas I wove around myself that year despite the unlikely, lonely, goofiness of the task, despite anything my College Professional Standards Committee might say when I returned and submitted a sabbatical report. The words Lorenzo sent were impossible. "Quasi-steel, Chiasma, Seduction, Plastic,

Myth, and Hair." His sestina, "Suspended Things," is probably the emptiest, most cacophonous poem I ever wrote. There's a sniper in it looking from "the window of a quasi-steel/ hotel" through his range finder—"twin hairs/ meeting in a menacing chiasma."

CAROLYN

I met my most eminent word-donor when she visited my campus as a guest of our Women's Studies program. Carolyn Heilbrun, distinguished Columbia professor, feminist critic, and pseudonymous mystery-writer, became interested in my project:

> Dear Sarah,
>
> Of course I'm terrifically busy ... but I like your game and wanted to send off my greetings and my six words ... most unpoetic but [they] are the concepts I'm living with at the moment. They surface, in fact, in my next detective novel which will be out in March or April and is called *Sweet Death, Kind Death* from a poem of Stevie Smith's. Anyway, the words are Death, Friend, Marriage, Biography, Conversation, Story ... In my mind they none of them mean what we have mainly or conventionally assumed them to mean ... Why did you pick Montreal to be lonely in, I wonder ... don't trouble to answer by mail ...

Carolyn's *nom de plume* for mystery novels was Amanda Cross, and her sestina is "Tibi Quae Amanda Est," "you who are to be loved." (Come to think of it, the verb should be *Es*, not *Est*.) Anyway, Carolyn was indeed loved by many friends despite her sometimes unforgiving views of biography and story.

> In letters or in leaves, biographies
> are blown away as precious conversations
> among characters, men and women friends,
> like those I lose when your story
> ends…

Easy enough to bend and stretch some of Carolyn's words. But Death? What else does that mean but itself? I remembered Saint Francis, who had greeted Death as his Sister. He believed that Faith would deliver him from the "Death after Death." As far as I know, Carolyn did not hold that belief any more than I do. As far as I know, the people she left behind when she took her own life in 2003 found Death to mean exactly what it's conventionally assumed to mean: radical absence, separation from near loves.

Owen

My younger son managed to find his way from Amherst to Montreal for a visit. It was lovely to see him and have him as a guest in my furnished studio apartment. I remember how impressed he was by the water pressure in the shower ("strong enough to stop a Peace March!").

During his time with me, he met acquaintances of mine who praised my ingenuity at inventing and executing the Sestina Game. "I don't see what's so hard about it," he said. "OK, you try." And Owen, who had strenuously avoided literary study of any kind, promised he would try, but returned to school without my having assigned his words. He came up with his own, and soon I received them in the mail. (Someone must have explained that he didn't need a Canadian stamp.) His first, and probably last, sestina recalls his years of floundering through adolescence in my care. Reading it fills me with pain, pride, and parental remorse. What a good title he chose:

"take this"

> Because this was to be an experiment
> I have been made into an engineer.
> no sweat, though hampered by years of smoking grass
> so imagine this scene
> and take it with proverbial salt
> and it will speak about our character.

In a sestina, each end-word gets a turn to be repeated (at the end of one stanza and the beginning of the next).

> Something has always been plastic in my character
> partly because I'm a result of your experiment.

Never in those hard years had I seen Owen as my experiment, but now I had to accept that he saw things that way. The engineer in the first stanza is himself; in the second it's me—"you the engineer" worrying about "rockets made with potassium salt" by him and his buddies, whose pranks went far beyond those suggested in chemistry sets.

The kid is a grown man now, doing well. Why transcribe here his middle stanzas? They allude to "wounds that opened" during the early years and were still open at the time he wrote. He keeps the six balls in the air: our experiments, our character, his grass ("you cut the grass/ that I should have mowed"), his sadness, though he balances blame with applause for a certain gallantry in my parenting and in my zany game:

> I always thought you were a good engineer, Mom.

> These poems are a good experiment and your character
> does well to engineer such therapeutic scenes.
> but salt does not affect the grass's growth.

Well, yes it does, and he knew it, but chose to end the poem on a note of reconciliation.

Meanwhile, he gave me the words he wanted me to put in a poem for him (Vodka, Fathom, Silk, Drop, Stain, Force). The result was too awkward to record, and Malcolm, Owen's older brother, never sent words, though we talked pretty often on the phone.

As Owen's poem showed, sestinas, far from being especially difficult, are ideal beginner poems. Inexperienced poets need a frame to hang the words on, and a guiding structure. It's quite easy to put end-words in their proper order along the right hand side of a page:

(1) experiment

(2) engineer

(3) grass

(4) scene

(5) salt

(6) character

Then, as in a spiral, 6 becomes 1, 1 becomes 2, 5 becomes 3, 2 becomes 4, 4 becomes 5, and 3 becomes 6:

> character
>
> experiment
>
> salt
>
> engineer
>
> scene
>
> grass

and so on for 36 lines (medieval manuals called this *retrogradatio crociata*) until, were there to be a seventh stanza, the endings would return in the original order. But instead of continuing ad infinitum, you wrap things up with a three-line envoi using all six of the end-words, two in each line, with three at the ends of the lines, the others where you will. Once you have ends for all the lines, you need only write 39 beginnings and middles.

It's not the form itself that's difficult. It's taking six unlikely words and inveigling them into a poem with some life and music in it. This is very seldom accomplished. In the rare great sestina, such as Elizabeth Bishop's about the *grandmother,* the *almanac,* and the *Little Marvel stove,* the words acquire so much resonance, and the whole becomes so expressive, that the reader almost forgets what form is in play.

Many readers dislike the sestina for its artifice and monotony. I have written very few since overdosing on them all those years ago. True, there must be some value, some mysterious magic, to a pattern still practiced after a thousand years, in a climate different in nearly every respect from Arnaut Daniel's.

But to write sixteen sestinas one after the other was asking too much of the form. Only three were published in magazines, and of those there's only one I still like to read all the way through (Sue Ellen Holbrook's "Plum"). But readable or not, the project prevented me from going mad with loneliness. It kept me functioning, learning, and in touch with friends, at least while I worked on their words, inhabited their worlds, and provisionally assumed their interests and sympathies.

An economist colleague, Jack Amariglio, sent words evoking his heady world of Marxist theory, which I began to explore, although in the end, reading Brecht was about as far as I got.

Galileo and Other Renegades
Aphrodite raised her shaded star one April
right to the focal point of his desire.
He trained a lens, as was his practice
every night—a lens-line, at the time, the only bridge
connecting Venice to the scene of his critique.
He saw that Venus, like the moon, is not the origin
of her own light. There had to be another origin.

Other interests of Jack's—jazz, baseball—got wedged into the poem. John Ashbery could have managed it, not me.

So, enough *retrogradatio cruciata*.

But why sestinas? Why Arnaut Daniel? Why troubadours? A reason, please.

This *razo* begins in the recesses of my earliest *amor de lonh*.

II
MY MOTHER'S COMET

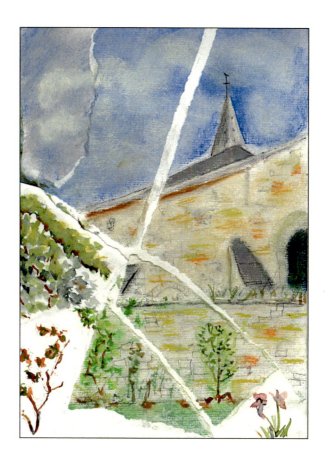

"The Sea Bird"

My poems are rarely even the least abstract. Often straightforward narratives of an identifiable incident, they don't require *razos*. So the *razos* in this section are meant to explain not the poems, but my vocation for far love—which I acquired from my mother, Martha, and she from her mother, Grace.

Martha's first near love was her father, Fred Hawley, but he became a far love when Grace left him, taking seven-year-old Martha to Europe along with Wawa (Laura), the nurse. Then Wawa became Martha's near love, and Grace another far one, roaming about to seek loves of her own and, failing that, games of baccarat. My Grandma frequented posh casinos in Atlantic City and Biarritz, craving action on green baize tables. In one of my poems, my mother becomes

The Sea Bird

With Mama and Wawa
and Louis Vuitton, she sailed
when she was 7.

She sang Aunt Rhody's
old gray goose with Mama,
the gayest goose she knew.
The century was seven too.

Grace was a restless woman who couldn't bear waiting around if things were not going well for her. She didn't wait around to make a home for Martha, who grew up in a series of hotel suites, homeless except when staying with her Aunt and Uncle in their country house near Bayonne, France. Nor did Grace wait around for me to be born. I knew only her portrait, hers

and Martha's, which hung on the wall in our dining room.
There, I saw Grace pose in fake garden scenery (at the time I
didn't know it was fake), wearing a pouf of "ratted" silver hair, a
black and cream lace décolletage, and a smile that suggested she
meant to play the role of some sort of mother to the ten-year-
old girl nestled in the crook of her arm, placed there by the
painter, because (as I later learned) mother and daughter never
posed together. Martha wears a knowing scowl, a pleated frock,
a floppy taffeta hair-bow. On her lap she holds an open score.
Wagner. The Love-Death scene from Tristan, Martha told
me at times, though other times she said it was the Siegfried
Idyll—either bliss-filled birth or orgasmic death.

> They sailed to France and back,
> and sailed again,
> with Halley's Comet overhead.
> The century was 10.

> Aboard the "Lafayette"
> she posed.
> I see her hair-bow flutter
> like a little puff of feathers.

> What do I read in her face
> there on the deck of the Lafayette,
> sailing either east or west
> in a blue serge sailor dress?

> She knows, of life, I guess,
> What Maisie Knew,
> more or less.

Martha also liked to tell me about the comet and how frightened she'd been in 1910 as it approached perihelion. Playing on the Champs-Elysées, she saw picture postcards of Halley's striking Earth, splitting it into fiery chunks that went tumbling off through space. No serious people thought the Earth would be destroyed in this way, but one French astronomer did claim that masses of people would die from the cyanide gasses in the tail. Martha's fear was that the catastrophe would strike at a time when she and Grace were apart. She confided the fear to no one and fretted to the point of illness. But then, she said, Mother arrived and all was well.

> "On my birthday,
> in Vevey, over the Alps
> we saw the comet.
> I'll never forget it!"

This reunion of mother and daughter in a backdrop of mountains and comet mixes fact with fiction. Martha's birthday fell in late July, by which time, in 1910, Halley's Comet was no longer visible to the naked eye.

Facts about Halley's Comet: Its dusty tail contains not cyanide, but ice. When closest to the Sun, a few tons of its crystal hair melt, so each time around, the comet becomes smaller and will eventually disappear.

> Song of the Egret of Grace
> She will take my feather.
> She will wear a hat.
>
> She will have a box.
> That will not spoil the feather.

Comets are always either approaching or receding, but even when a comet is "near" the Earth, the two bodies are an enormous distance apart, like Grace and Martha, like Martha and me.

> It will travel with her
> in the holds of steamers
>
> through Atlantic weather
> with a dozen others.
>
> It is made of leather.
> She will wear the hat.
>
> It will have my feather.
> I will tell her daughter.

Grace, in my view, was a silly woman. I like to think my mother's ten-year-old scowl expresses her refusal to grow up to be as silly as her mother. She tried to turn out less vain, improvident, and drifting. She learned better French than her mother or her aunts. She studied and read in two languages. She learned to paint extremely well. When she married and had two children, she stopped painting, unfortunately, but resolved to do a better job of mothering than Grace had, to give me and my brother a home, and wait around while we grew up. Such resolutions to improve on a previous generation are often made (I've made them myself), but often the vow merely drives the old pattern a little deeper. From the time I was born until the time I went to school, surrogate caretakers were my near loves, and my parents far ones. The pattern seemed to rule not only Martha's character, but the outside world as well. By the time I was ten, the second of her world wars had come and gone, taking with it two men of our family, and those events, as well as her own inclination, drew her back to France, where she spent at least three months each year looking after bereaved relations—she, a lovely widow on her side of the Atlantic, I, a longing schoolgirl, on mine.

> 'Long'
> Extending
> through distance, having
> greater
> than usual
> height, a vowel
> of long
> duration
> A in Fate, E in Equal
>
> Extending
> in reach, a fighter's long left jab—
> the long
> I
> in Flight
>
> To long, from too long, tedious, long to have greater
> than usual reach, to hear *the long voice*
> of the hounds,
> the O in Go.

When she was in France, she thrived on my adoring letters. When she returned, she was wounded by my cool welcome and sulky ways. I looked so much like the grouchy girl in the portrait that people thought, despite the Edwardian décor, that its subjects were my mother and me. I was puzzled by my own response to Martha. She was so charming, called me such affectionate names, and had suffered so much grief in her life. But she had become my far love, and I couldn't shift her back to being my near one. Many people have trouble with that shift. The troubadours, for example, never made it. It was far love they needed most. I need both, but when given the choice, I've tended to take far.

I, Who Never Learned to Long

For the troubadours, longing was loving in its noblest form.
Love-from-Afar made words into poems, made melodies rise
from the score.

Soon after the Last World War,
my widowed mother traveled to France every year
leaving me in the care of Sadie, the Maid.

When I wasn't in school, I would play in the park
and a neighbor would say:
"I'll bet you'll be glad when your mother comes home."

Of course, you old bat, I'll be glad when she's home,
glad to be shown her new French clothes, glad to hear
of her afternoons on the shores of the River Adour.

When the Traveler returned, she told everybody how happy
we were, she and I, and, at the time,

I believed her.

Map of France II

Among the five rivers
—*S e i n e & M a r n e,*
                    R
                           h
&   *ô*
L   *n*
 o   *e*
  i
   r
    e,

        lord of them all,
I saw her
            in Hermès silk
                @ Paris
      A *château-fleuve*
    to the South the sky
      blue light
    from
the *Basses Pyrénées* her address
        near Pau
near Saint-
John
of
Light

    a r o n n e   *G a r o n*
G   *n e*

Once a girl has seen across
    the blind Atlantic
        and heard—above its roar . . .
           a far-off love is born.

Girls and Wars ("The Sea Bird," cont'd)

She knew there had been a war in France thirty years before she was born. She knew France had lost because Huns were beasts. After the war, they were still beasts, but they ran a tight ship, and she was aboard one of them—the *Amerika*, with a K—when the first of her wars broke out. The ship had to turn around in mid-Atlantic because France and England were blockading the Channel and no German ship could dock at Southampton or Le Havre. It was August 1914.

This was hard on Martha. America with a C held no home for her, and no school. Wars were horrid. What would become of her beloved Aunt and Uncle, who lived in France?

"This is Aunt Julia," said Grace to Martha. The toddler looked up at her slight, fair aunt, mouthed the word "Odoody," and "Odoody" the woman remained for the whole family, in stories my mother told about her to anyone who would listen. In my mind, those anecdotes made my grandmother's younger sister sound very neurotic and odd: a girl who had taken to her bed at the drop of a hat and tyrannized the household with mysterious ailments; a young woman whose chronic malaise so stymied her doctor that he said he could do nothing for her, and recommended that she become a Christian Scientist, which she did, adopting the beliefs of Mary Baker Eddy, another odd woman. That same doctor recommended that Julia's reproductive organs be disabled, which they were, or so everyone thought. Perhaps doctors performed a mock hysterectomy as some sort of exorcism, because, at age 40, Odoody was operated on for appendicitis, found to be pregnant, and quickly sewn up again. I thought stories like these suited a person named Odoody. But there was a tragic story about the death of her son, and I wondered how that could be. Would the worst thing that could happen to anyone happen to a person with a name that sounded like what dogs do in the flower beds?

Martha told stories, odd and sad, about Odoody and Uncle Charles, which she pronounced "Sharl," the portrait-painter Julia Anderson married in 1910 in Paris, where she had gone to study singing though "she had no voice." I heard endlessly about this Aunt and Uncle, saw their photographs, their silverware monogrammed JAW, and Uncle Charles's paintings—varnished academic affairs untouched by any influence of Modernist, Impressionist, or *fauve*. I absorbed the lore of these far loves of Martha's. It was as if she wanted to embed their lives in my brain, knowing that one day, her own brain would fail and those beloved lives would otherwise lose all meaning. Did they have any meaning to begin with? How could I know while she was so assiduously describing them, displacing my own impressions with her own, filling my nervous system with her memories and wars?

"I saw the comet.
I'll never forget it!"

Then she forgot it.
I wrote, and read aloud,
some tales that she had told.

Aboard *Amerika* (with a K)
you watched the gulls' cotillion,
and heard a War had just begun.
The century was 14.

"Go tell Aunt Rhody right away!"
You had to double back
to plain America
and couldn't go to school in France.

It often seems to me that Martha is dictating these pages. Nonetheless, I resolve that from now on, there is to be no "Odoody." Her name was Julia Anderson Willems. Oddly or not, she conceived a child in 1915, which shocked her American family—an older brother, his wife, and their sister, Grace. Julia was 40, allegedly frail, married to a minor *artiste* who did not strike his American relatives as particularly competent. Grace was dispatched to Paris, where the birth would take place. Paris, so near the front, and besieged by the terrible Huns.

At Miss Bennett's School, in Millbrook, New York, Martha was alone in the spot where Grace had ensconced her in 1914, after the return of the *Amerika*. None of her schoolmates shared her involvement with French events—trench warfare, *les poilus,* poison gas. Alone, the fifteen-year-old awaited news of the three most important people in the world. And the cable came: Joy in war-torn Paris. A Perfect Boy.

Across the tree

...I'll draw a dotted line
between two cousins:

Martha, b. 1900 in St. Louis
Frederick, b. 1916 in Paris
under zeppelins
and evil stars.

She didn't meet the miraculous child until after the war. He was 2, still perfect, blond like his mother, sturdy and spoiled like his father, naughty with nurses, tender with Julia, conspiratorial with his pretty cousin Martha. She was sixteen years older than he but half a generation younger than his parents. Two onlies, they became devoted allies.

> They travelled
> in one another's countries.
> She was sister to him,
> mother, almost lover.

After these lines, my poem "Across the Tree" skips more than 20 years, leaping, as a poem can, to a new war that began when Frederick was 23. His parents hoped he would take advantage of his dual citizenship and go live safely in America, but he felt himself French and had a sense of chivalry—or in any case, of cavalry, the branch of the army he chose because he liked to ride. From September 1939 to May 1940 his unit was stationed in Flanders. That winter and spring of the Phony War, his letters, written from the impregnable Maginot Line, sounded as if he, his men, and the horses were enjoying themselves. Then came June, which "Across the Tree" pretends to remember with its panicked letters, cables, news, and tears.

> And when he died at 24
> from a bullet through the eye,
>
> > Mort pour la France
> > *sur le coup et sans souffrance* ...

In fact, I was not quite four and don't remember, but letters kept coming up to the time when my memory kicks in—airmail, grief for my first cousin once and forever removed.

… the news flew over
 in envelopes
with chevron borders.
She opened them

And wept.
I tried to fathom
her lovely tears. I wanted
to collect them,
divert the stream,

and I grew mean
over a blond, dead boy
who whispered to my mother
in two tongues

At home in upstate New York, Edmund, my father, waited until the United States had entered the war so he could enter it too, though he didn't have to. He was 38, father of two, and in poor health. But he, too, had been raised in a household mourning its war heroes. One of his older brothers had been killed at Gallipoli, the other scarred in a fiery dogfight over France. And I think my father was as jealous as I was of Freddie, who'd had the luck to occasion so much grief in Martha. For these and other reasons, my father enlisted in 1941 despite age, asthma, and congenital heart trouble. The Army Air Corps never sent him oversees but stationed him in far-off Georgia, where he ran the post exchange of a training camp. Even that stress was too much for him, and he was medically discharged in 1944. He came home, still sick, around V-E Day, celebrated the end of the war with us in August, and died in September. My brother had just turned fifteen, and I was turning nine. Martha, of course, gave Edmund a solemn burial (keeping the folded flag) but never shed as many tears for him as for Frederick. Eddie, Bill, and I were her near loves, and we all wished we could have been her far one.

In France, a florist

tended Frederick's tomb,
just for the money,
decking the stones
with bloodless roses—

My ally, Monsieur Gelos.

More Girls and Wars

A girl ties herself to a mast to keep from steering toward islands where she might hear more war songs. The damp ropes hold, but siren music enters her unstopped ears. Homer's sirens, it is said, were the monk seals barking along the reefs of the Li Galli islands, but even supposing that's what they were, if the girl sailed by, she would hear songs of her war.

Tip-toe, in Mother's victory garden,
she seeks a sky-borne silhouette,
perhaps her favorite—
twin-tailed P-38.

Far-off, Father knows his girl
has learned the Air Corps silhouettes.

He's far-off. She is resigned.

> One day, he's home
> but goes again, and stays away.
> This fills her brain.
>
> She knows it's wrong.
> She's one of many girls
> with many fathers, yet
> no war but hers exists.

In a few years, few living souls will know there were victory gardens, plane spotting, or P-38's, and the girl's little poem will not mean a thing. But she shouts that her war must not be forgotten. Her mother did not let *her* forget. Why should she let others crowd out her war with theirs?

In January 1991, she sat beside Mother's bed in the nursing home. Nearby TVs roared and reddened with flaming oil rigs, but the old woman, who had lost her sight, exclaimed, "Thank God there are no wars anymore!" She was only blind, not deaf. She knew very well what she was hearing. There were still wars, and a new one, a "Gulf War," had begun. What her mother meant was that there were no more wars as great as hers, none with the power to bereave as she and her dear aunt had been bereft.

Shadows

The poet Robert Desnos died in a prison camp just before the end of the Second World War. He addressed *Le dernier poème* to his wife:

> I have dreamed so much of you
> that I have become a shadow among shadows

a hundred times more shadow than the shadow …
the shadow that comes and goes
in your illuminated life.

It struck me as the key in which to write a poem about Julia.

Julia Willems, Her Son at War

May he not die.
May he not crawl into a shadow and die.
May the shadow be sent to me.

May he die and think a brave lie.
May the truth be sent to me.

May he not die seeing another woman's child shoot
    him in the eye.
May he not die shooting another woman's child in the eye.

And may no other woman's child survive him.

MAP OF FRANCE III

Wondrous were the syllables my declining mother strung together!

What was the name of the gardener with a club foot who buried the silver?

A farmer carried letters East
to Pau—miles from the château—

folded in his boot—
I knew his name. Did she want that?

Or censors' names in Lisbon
who tore them, taped them up again,

and let them go—
private woe

in envelopes with chevron borders
for Britton the postmaster

to slip into our box at home—
a number I remembered,

with Saint Martin, patron
of a village near Bayonne

where Lafourcade the farmer
farmed. No, it was the gardener's

name she wanted and I found it for her—
Broquedise—but never found the silver.

Decades went by before I could travel in France unburdened by this stuff. On the first trip, I was seventeen and traipsed behind Martha—first to Paris, where I sat in on dress-fittings *chez* Jacques Heim, relished my first croissant, and became enamored of the Cluny Museum's Unicorn Lady. In Biarritz, I met the legendary "Uncle Sharl," a widower by then who had painted nothing for years but his own wrinkled face, with pancake makeup. He wore a matted hairpiece and flirted grotesquely, tapping my mother on the behind, ogling my legs whenever I wore shorts. His Basque domestics, Noélie and Pierre, were the only other "French" people I met. The rest were elderly Brits and Americans from the Willemses' dwindling circle of expatriates.

On subsequent trips, I continued to carry Martha's map, once deliberately to trace the family and get the war stories out of my system—that was in the 1990s. My research guided me to the old château (though not to the silver) and to the site where Frederick's remains had lain since the end of the war, exhumed from the Norman village where he was killed, transported to Biarritz's *Cimetière de Sabao*. Now all three Willemses lie under the pink marble block and huge white cross chosen by Frederick's sad mother. I noted the Gelos flower shop nearby and threw away the frayed, weather-washed synthetic blossoms I found on the site. I was the last family member who would ever visit the tomb or even know it's there.

> This is why I wash the tombs
> of those who mourned him.
> They mourn no longer. Their distress
> is gone, but I must come
>
> to them. I'm on to other dooms
> and have other fish
> to fry tomorrow but I'll wash the tombs
> and fix a picnic. Everybody comes.

I took the whole morbid, lonely trip just to collect a few things to tell her about the things she'd told me.

She drowsed. I read:

"You were at sea.

"The War! the school!
Nothing to do
but settle in your cabin,
and read Innocents Abroad."

My mother sat up in a flurry:

"Oh! I loved that story."

Map of France IV

"We have written to Tarbes."

Then I began to follow my own maps to places that would have surprised her—Auvillar, Moissac, Toulouse. I had other fish to fry in southwest France, and rarely thought of the Willemses. But, once, as friends drove me on an excursion from Toulouse to St. Bertrand de Comminges, I was transfixed by a name on the road signs: "Tarbes." I recalled a letter my mother had shown me. June, 1940. Frederick's parents were trying to locate his unit after the Maginot Line *débâcle*. They had written, Aunt Julia said, to the Swiss Red Cross, and "we have written to Tarbes." I wanted François and Marie to stop the car. I wanted to tell them I'd had a cousin. He had gone to cavalry school in Tarbes. He'd been killed in Normandy in 1940—ten years, at least, before they were born, and I needed to tell my two French friends what a terrible war it had been.

Pietà

There is something sinister in the Reasons for my poems about the Willemses and the war—something to do with the state I was in when I first heard the stories, and with their persistence in my life. My mother recorded them for me on cassette tapes, but that was unnecessary. There was already a tape running in my head: "we have written to Tarbes," "*sur le coup et sans souffrance,*" "our immeasurable sorrow," Broquedise, Lafourcade, St. Martin de Seignanx. Decades before I became a mother myself, I was sucked into the maternal anguish of a great-aunt I never knew. I can still read what she wrote on July 24, 1940, my mother's fortieth birthday—"I know all your hearts are aching with ours." The letter, having said what it needed to say to my mother, should have been destroyed. I should never have seen it. It has prevented me from understanding that or any other war. Julia's phrases congeal into a hulking monument, a larger than life-sized marble woman with a stone corpse on the drapery of her stone knees. The figure looms, absorbs all the light that might illumine millions of Mothers, *Madres, Mütter* … and make them matter.

Bullet Couplets

I sing the bullet that struck a soldier in the eye.
I sing the soldier, who would "instantly and painlessly" die

for France according to a letter written
by his captain from a German prison.

The soldier was my cousin. I was four.
I didn't know him though I knew there was a war.

Eighty years have passed. I often read the note in
 which the captain
tells a mother what has happened

to her only son: He was shot for France's sake,
slept suddenly, and would never wake,

never be captured or imprisoned, never know
that France surrendered and began a long collaboration

with the enemy. I sing a mother and a son—
she, inconsolable, he, the lucky one.

III
PATHS TO OC

Consequentia Rerum

Most American poets who read troubadours do so because of Ezra Pound. Pound read them because of Dante. Many of my contemporaries found Dante on Pound's extensive reading list, then trekked further down the list to look at troubadours. For me the route was slightly different: first Dante, then troubadours, then Pound. But why Dante?

When I went to college, my heart's desire was to be a poet, but I wasn't a poet and couldn't imagine how to become one. I consoled myself by learning Italian and enrolling in a course on Dante, and the *Commedia* became a new heart's desire. I hoped for the rest of my life to keep reading that divine encyclopedia. The man who opened its door for me was Charles Singleton, heir to a distinguished line of scholars in Harvard's Dante Chair, first held by Longfellow, then James Russell Lowell, later by Charles Grandgent, Singleton's immediate predecessor and editor of my edition of the *Commedia*. Grand Gent indeed! "Names are the consequence of things," says Dante.

It's because of Dante (though ultimately because of my mother) that my study and practice of poetry have been so skewed toward romance languages rather than the language I live in—skewed toward my far loves and away from the near and dear one. A friend once told me my poems sounded like translations from another language.

The Parting of the Robes

Late last November,
your tawny gown and my plum-red one
sewn hem to hem
kept us warm

April is cold in the red silks alone

sounds like false Japanese.

Ten years after graduating from the college once called Radcliffe, I went to grad school at the University of Michigan to get certified for high-school French teaching. I never received the certificate. I fled from pattern drills, quizzes, ditto machines, and fifteen-year-olds into the safety of seminar rooms. In my doctoral program, I chose the medieval period as my specialty. I wanted the most distant possible refuge from my own life and times, and I needed another excuse to read Dante. It was on my second trip through the *Commedia* that I stopped to acquaint myself with troubadours. I was curious to learn why Dante, as an apprentice, had studied troubadours, and why, as a mature poet, he had placed a troubadour in each of his three divine realms. It occurs to me now that by introducing and describing them in Hell, Purgatory, and Paradise, he was writing a kind of *razo* for each one, extrapolating from their poems and *vidas* a commentary to guide future readers of their songs.

I've always found Arnaut to be the most compelling Commedia troubadour.

Arnaut Daniel Speaks His Reasons

I sing for the usual reasons ...
because branches are budding
and tree-tops
are coloring with many flowers,
greening with leaves,
and the songs and calls

>   of birds fill shady spots
>   of the forest.

Puois que, because, also contains the idea of time, "post," which begins as temporal and ends up causal—*post hoc ergo propter hoc*—not always a fallacy. "I sing *since* the branches are budding," and

>   because [*pel,* this time] of the song in the forest
>   and in order that no one reproach me
>   I work and smooth
>   worthy words
>   with the skills of Love,
>   from which I can't sever my heart.

Those are the basic occasions for the poem. You can take them as given and recognize them from now on when I repeat them with variations. (*D'autra guiza e d'autra razon*) ...

>   In another way and on another theme
>   and differently from usual, I must sing.
>   Don't think that from my pain
>   I hope to make a good, sweet song.

Given that my honor as a poet-lover, as well as the weather and the birds, make me sing, I must explain that this particular song will be harsh and difficult because, at the moment, love itself is harsh and difficult:

>   I hope to make a good song
>   but I have to ask many people's forgiveness
>   for singing about the one who does me wrong ...

Between the lady's behavior, and that of the mischief-makers around us, my many efforts are in vain. She resists me the way hard wood resists the plane, and snarled hair refuses the comb, and precious materials defy the artisan. But I persist (because of love, the weather, and … did I mention the birds?). Struggle is my mainspring.

In the world's first sestina, I struggle to *enter* a *chamber* and a *soul* defended by an *uncle* with a *nail* and a *rod*. The siege is exhausting but wondrous. How many others have sung so well such unkempt words? Just try writing six stanzas using terms like those at the ends here—

> The firm desire that enters
> my heart won't be deterred by the beak or the fingernail
> of a flatterer whose gossip will cost him his soul.
> I don't dare beat him up with a branch or rod,
> (not openly), but, out there where lives no uncle
> of mine, I'll enjoy myself in an orchard or chamber.

What with the gossips I mentioned earlier, I often resort to speaking in code about my plight, declaring my identity openly but not my precise situation or the futile strategies I employ.

> I am Arnautz who gathers air,
> chases the hare with the ox
> and swims against the current.

These lines are encrypted, but enough of my listeners have the key so I can reference the lines and show later developments in my life as a poet-lover.

> Love and joy and place and time
> return my mind
> to that trouble I had a year or so ago
> when I hunted the hare with the ox.
> Now it goes worse and better for me in love,
> for I love well (and for that call myself lucky)
> but don't have any certainty of joy
> if Love and pleading don't conquer her hard heart ...

and here ...

> Before the top branches
> of trees remain dry or leafless ...

Soon the trees will have dried out and lost their greenery, but old age is no excuse.

> Love still commands me
> to sing a brief song with a long theme
> (*breu chansson de razon loigna* ...)

You'll have noticed that *razo* means not just "reason" but "topic," and, at times, "rule" or "method," the kind of thing one learns in school. Once a student, always a student. My own school is one in which Love is the teacher and the principal.

> ... he's taught me so well the arts of his school
> that I know how to stop the current,
> and my ox can outrun the hare ...

Get it? No? Too bad. That's all you'll hear about my life or my reasons. Until I die, that is.

Then scribes and commentators will come and explain in prose why I wrote such difficult songs. Their explanations will be crude, without nuance or irony. It will be suggested that my ox (*bou*) owed its existence to the surname (Bouville) of my lady's husband (Madame Bouville? Never heard of her!) and that I stole one of my songs from a mere *jongleur*. No one believes those stories. Everyone admires me. Even the great Dante. I can tell a few stories about him.

He got many of his ideas from me. He imitated my voice in songs about some difficult love of his.

> ***Così nel mio parlar voglio esser aspro ...***
>
> Thus, in my speech I want to be as harsh
> as the acts of that lovely stone lady hardened
> by ever more harshness and cruelty,
> who puts on such armor
> that because of it
> no arrow from any quiver
> can strike her naked skin.

From me he learned the flinty struggle between delicate feelings and indelicate verbal material. (Mind you, it's more difficult to sing harshly in Italian than in Occitan.) Then, a hundred years after my death, when he visited Hell, he would remember my "unkempt words" and use them to describe a wilderness of sin, *questa selva selvaggia ed aspr'e forte.*

While on that pilgrimage he reached Purgatory, and the two of us met face to face ... on the Terrace of the Lustful—where else?

I had already spent ninety years in the flames. It took only ten to climb the lower terraces and be purged of six other sins.

Those early years were the worst. I had nothing in common with the souls I met—no friends among the Sloths, Profligates, Gluttons, or Enviers. But in these flames I've felt at home. Here we, the "lustful according to Nature" (in other words, heterosexuals) daily embrace the "unnatural" Sodomites who circle the mountain in the opposite direction. They remind me of my old gay friends, Truc Malec and Raimon Durfort, with whom, in youth, I engaged in obscene debates at the expense of a certain Lady Aymon.

On the seventh terrace there are two paths. Closest to the mountain wall, the path is covered in perpetual fire, while the other, near the edge, stays cool and clean. I take care not to stray from the fire. But one afternoon, I noticed a few orange flames darkening to crimson. I looked toward the Western sky and saw, on the cooler path, a man standing with the afternoon sun behind him. He was casting a shadow as if still alive, which he was. I looked at him, ceased to feel the usual effect of fire on my skin, and understood that my body was an illusion, immune to pain.

The shadow-man addressed me with one of those figures that weaves a tortuous garland around its message. "The desire of his mind," he said, "had prepared a gracious lodging for my name." In plain words, "who was I"?

My heart (my real heart) began to burn and respond to the questioner in my own Occitan, but with words unlike any I'd spoken before:

> *Tan m'abellis vostre cortes deman*
> *qu'ieu no me puesc ni voill a vos cobrire.*

> (Your courteous invitation so pleases me
> that I cannot and will not conceal myself from you)

It was not the old Arnaut Daniel who sang those bland, benevolent, and biteless verses. The old Arnaut prided himself on mixing confession with concealment, and could never have sung:

> *Ieu sui Arnautz que plor e vau cantan.*

Yet it was true. I was weeping, singing and circling in a current of fellow souls. Where were the ox and the hare of my difficult love? Incredulous, I continued to speak words I had heard from a few fellow troubadours at the ends of their lives:

> With sorrow I see my past folly ...
> I had scorned and pitied them as limp old monks, but now I felt no scorn.
> ... joyfully I see the joy I hope for, tomorrow.

The word "Joy" I had sung before, but never "tomorrow," never "hope"! For me, Joy was now or never. That day, I added my prayer to that of the others ... to be remembered by the pilgrim when he reached the end of his journey. Then, noticing that I'd moved out of the flames, I ended my plea and dropped back into the ardent stream. The poet would describe his last sight of me just as I was "hidden ... by refining fire."

Alighieri and I will not meet again. By the time he returns, shadowless, to this terrace to be shriven of his Lust, I'll have risen to the place prepared for me—revolving, singing, gazing up from my seat in the circle of the Moon (a planet I never mentioned in my songs). A bath in Lethe will have erased all memory of the hare and the bull, of Truc Malec, of Lady Aymon

and the others, all thought of my joys, treats, sins, poems, too
… drowned in a swell of hymns.

Postscript

We souls see into the future. Six centuries from now, my songs will be revealed to the New World by an ambitious young poet writing in the lingo of *yes*. He will attempt to renew that tongue. By giving his fellow poets lessons in *oc* and *si,* he will teach "The Spirit of Romance." He will misread my signature line

> *Ieu soi Arnaut che amas l'aura*

and write, "I am Arnaut who *loves* the air." Absurd. If I'd loved plentiful, sweet air, I wouldn't have chased the hare with a bull or swum against the current (he got those lines right.) It was the struggle to "*gather* (*amasar*) the air" and to grasp other unattainable objects that prompted all my poems.

The Trouble with Arnaut Daniel

His match recall and switch game
worms its way to your brain.

Beaks in a bush
hone love to the size
of a stick or chessboard—

Cheeseboard? Tropes.
Ropes. Rules.

Rods have souls. Uncle
comes with fingernails, says *Enter,*
and seals the chamber.

I am Arnaut!
is heard
in the current. You

go mute or write
lines on How to gather air
without a net.

Dante's One and Only Reason

L'amor che nella mente mi ragiona …
Love that speaks its reasons in my mind …

The New Life

Things are reasons
for names, bridges between
the rose and the word

"suffuse." A Verb
causes Beatrice
to cross the bridge in her crimson gown,

synonymous
with Nine. Time
tolls. The lad, stunned,

greets her friend,
Giovanna, and
the occasion, Christ. He knows

Eros lives
on a road to some
Tuscan estate.

> He chooses Caritas,
> a naked child
> who furtively
>
> consumes his heart.

The title of Dante's poetic autobiography should be written in red. (Perhaps it is. I've never seen the manuscripts.) He calls it *una rubrica,* a red ink chapter heading in the book of his days on Earth: *Incipit Vita Nova,* "A New Life Begins." One sees, in medieval Bibles and Psalters, red and black ink alternating to separate commentary from text, but if that procedure were strictly followed throughout *La Vita Nuova,* there must be too much red ink. Dante's verses—sonnets, ballads, *canzoni*—are all embedded in prose passages that give the reason, *ragione,* or occasion, *cagione,* for each composition. The reason is often longer than the poem itself and makes fully as great a claim on a reader's attention, perhaps because of Dante's great innovation—to write his own *razo,* using a compelling and authoritative first person. And most of the poems receive, in addition to a *razo,* a prose analysis similar to the *explication de texte* I tried to teach my students, dividing the poem into sections and giving the theme of each. The procedure seems terribly pedantic. I admit I usually skip these *divisioni.* It's as if in a musical, the actors paused not only to sing the song but also to explain what key it's in, what tempo, how many stanzas it has, and a summary of what each one has to say.

On the other hand, it's intriguing that a poet-narrator dares interrupt himself in this way, inviting us to read the *Vita Nuova* as a story—a Personal Anthology à la Borges—and as a handbook giving firsthand information about one man's practice and development. It shows the steps by which a skilled love poet became *the* poet of "Love that moves the Sun and the Other Stars."

Each step is important to Dante, but I'll describe the two most important to me.

Step I. From the Wish to the Will to Write

A misunderstanding has arisen between Dante and Beatrice, the Lady he worships. He relates the problem in detail, but here, it's enough to give the result. She withholds from him the precious gift of her greeting. Wordless greetings on a city street are all that ever occurs between these two. From their first meeting, when they are both nine years old, until the Lady dies, she is his far love (is he hers? we never learn that.). He was a normal young man and had near loves (in time, a wife and children), but these are excluded from this account of the love that rules his life, the one seen in a vision literally consuming his heart like a piece of fruit. So, when she withholds her "marvelous greeting," which up to now has warmed his whole life with the flame of Caritas, he is so grief-stricken that he can only hide, and bathe his hiding place with tears. As he weeps, the God of Love appears and suggests he write a ballad for Beatrice, assuring her of his lifelong devotion, and begging her to take pity. Love tells him exactly what each stanza of the ballata should contain. The poet transcribes the poem, and gives the typical analysis.

> This ballad is divided into three parts: In the first I tell it where it should go and encourage it in order for it to travel more confidently, and I tell it what company to seek if it wants to go safely and without danger. In the second I say what it needs to make itself understood.

In the third I allow it to return whenever it wishes, consigning its movements to the arms of fortune. The second part starts here: "With sweet sound …" The third here: "Gentle song …"[1]

Having answered a hypothetical objection to his use of the second person in the ballad, he returns to the love narrative. After completing the ballad, he pauses to reflect on Love. It is an enemy, he muses. It is also a friend—a paradox that Arnaut Daniel and other troubadours would have understood. To Dante, as to Arnaut before him, comes "the wish to write rhymed words" about love's difficulties. "And I composed this sonnet," says Dante, "which begins, 'All my thoughts.'" This is a list of love-tensions. The poet goes so far as to call his Lady his enemy, which might seem shocking were there not so many love poems that say the same thing. In the next poem, written after Beatrice has made fun of him in front of her friends, he calls her "murderer of his senses."

These are pretty good verses, but if Dante's poems had all been like them there would be no Dante chairs in universities. Perhaps he knew that, because at this point in the story, he lifts the level of his poetic aspiration, while telling us the reason, and a reason for the reason: It will, he says, be "delightful to hear."

Ladies of the city have noticed that he pales, grows faint, and flees whenever he sees Beatrice. They ask a question: "To what end [*a che fine*] do you love your lady when you cannot bear to be in her presence?" (a pithy formulation of far love). He answers, "Ladies, the purpose of my love used to be to gain this

---

[1] All translations from Dante's Vita Nova are taken from *Dante Vita Nuova: A New translation by Mark Musa.* Oxford, 1993.

lady's greeting, the object of all my desires. But ever since it pleased her to deny it, my lord Love has placed my blessedness in something which cannot fail me." Asked what this new aim might be, he answers that it is "to write words that praise my lady." He has been forced by Beatrice's behavior and by the probing ladies to evolve a theme loftier than that of the conventional love lyric with its laments, accusations, and pleas. His new resolve, he says, feels so new, so daring—perhaps too high an enterprise—that for several days, he remains torn between his "wish to compose" and his "fear of beginning." Dante actually allows his reader to imagine him—of all poets!—stymied over a blank page. Not for long.

Soon, things change in his relation to his one overriding reason. To be sure, she remains his far love. In fact, she will move farther away, farther even than the Countess of Tripoli from the troubadour Jaufre of Blaye. But from now on, his poetry will not depend on changes in the distance between them, only on his own determination to praise. The *voluntade de dire* becomes more than a mere *desiderio de dire*. It's not a *wish* but an active *will* to compose, and it takes his poetry to new and ecstatic heights. In the next canzone, he addresses only those who have an intelligent understanding of love—*donne ch'avete intelletto d'amore*. He speaks of angels. He speaks of bliss in the heaven to which Beatrice will soon be called. She is *disiata in sommo cielo*. These great stanzas, set at the center, require and receive a very long analysis.

Step 2: My Lady's Dead, Long Live My Lady

After the death occurs that he has foreseen, Dante grieves, and he compares his grief to that of Jeremiah's over Jerusalem. Dante's whole city has been bereaved like a widow (*quasi vedova*), despoiled of every worthwhile object. In weeping, he discovers a new and even more potent reason to write: "to vent his sadness in mournful words." Of course, as the reader has come to expect, he will have us read those words and his commentary on them. But he makes an interesting change in the procedure he has followed so far. As if newly afraid that a commentary after the poem may dilute the force of its lyricism, he announces that he will now place the analysis before the poem "in order that the song may remain more widowed [*più vedova*] at the end." He follows the changed order—analysis, then song—for the remainder of his little book.

One final movement advances the narrative toward its famous resolution. The occasion is another Lady. Dante's physical appearance has become distorted by all his grieving. He sees a noble gentlewoman in a window. She's observing him with pity. Grateful for her sympathy, he writes a sonnet praising her gentleness and discernment: "I realized you understood/ the nature of my dark life." He writes two more sonnets for the kind lady, and discovers that he has become, in his judgment, "too pleased to see her." He rebukes himself and, in tortuous terms, curses his own eyes:

> You used to look so sad that you made people weep. Now it seems you want to forget all that weeping for the sake of this lady who gazes at you. She gazes only in grief over the one you used to weep for. But let her gaze, because, seeing her, I will remember very often, my cursed eyes, that only in death should you cease weeping.

And he resolves to write a sonnet about this inner conflict, *questa battaglia*, between his far love and a possible near one. Even after he writes the sonnet, the battle for his soul continues. "Why," he asks himself, "don't you want to rescue yourself from such bitter tribulation?" He writes a new sonnet that resembles a troubadour debate, or *tenso*, between his soul and his heart. The heart speaks up in defense of "the new love spirit that responds to his desires." But the heart, "adversary of reason," is utterly vanquished by a vision of Beatrice at the age of their first meeting, wearing the blood-red robes she wore on that momentous day. Dante is struck by the memory and by the whole history of his devotion. Now all the days spent contemplating a new love appear as so many days of delusion and shame.

The sympathetic lady drops abruptly out of the story, still nameless and shadowy. I wish someone would write a novel about her and rescue her from the oblivion to which Dante consigns near love, defeated, hands down and for eternity, by the far one.

He will tell us in the *Convivio* that the unnamed lady was an allegorical figure: a Lady Philosophy similar to the one who visits Boethius in *The Consolation of Philosophy.* Beatrice, too, will become an allegorical figure whose complex meaning I am neglecting here in favor of the literal story Dante gives and, I think, never means his readers to discount. Love for the literal Beatrice defeats all affection for the literal Florentine Lady, and while this seems a cruel defeat (one that loomed over poetry for centuries!), it occurred because of Dante's choice of the best Reason for the best Poem. After far love wins the battle, he resolves to cease singing about any lady until such time as he can write of Beatrice "that which has never been written of any woman." And the rest, as they say, is *Commedia*.

The following sonnet is entitled "The Way Life Goes." I shall give the analysis first in order that the end may remain more widowy. The sonnet's turn, or *volta,* comes at line 9, "One time, she's surprised," which tells the exact moment when the near love described in lines 1 through 8 became a far one. Further divisions could be made, but I have already said too much.

The Way Life Goes

On elbows and knees
she takes the man in
who feels like a baker
the way he kneads.
After a moan, a span
of running around,
mixing it up, ordering
out. They resume.
One time, she's surprised
by two moans in a row, neither
stronger than the other,
nor more pained, it seems to her,
than tears behind her lens
when she walks against the wind.

The Puddle-Razo

I've changed my mind. I have to add to "The Way Life Goes" a commentary that belongs in this essay on Reasons and Writing.

Until recently, I took the troubadour tropes with a grain of salt and other spices: "If love goes well, you sing." "If love goes badly, you sing even more." I supposed that one troubadour or another had written and sung this because he meant it, and then all the others went about singing the same thing in different ways. As for the *razos*—written by authors distant in time and space from the songs themselves—I enjoyed their commentaries as early exercises in prose fiction, entertaining ways to misinterpret while claiming to explain. As for the *Vita Nuova,* I had dismissed the prose *libello* as a thin story concocted because Dante needed to organize a lot of love poems he had lying around, and because he preferred not to leave their interpretation in the hands of some hack *razo*-writer. I supposed he had selected 39 miscellaneous lyrics (some written for a girl named Beatrice, others not) and designated each one as a step toward his transcendent poetic goal. But the story itself and the psychic battle it described didn't grab me at all until my own life threw me back to his account of a choice, for reasons of poetic ambition, of far love over near.

I now need to report that the poems in my first book, and nearly all my own poems in this book, were written after the event described in lines 9 and 10 of "The Way Life Goes," an event that abruptly changed a four-year near love into an unending far one. It stuns me to realize that if I'm a poet at all, it's because of that event. I lost someone, and after that (*post hoc*), I wrote poems.

When Beatrice died, Dante was already a poet. So was Thomas Hardy when his Emma died, and, to cite one of my contemporaries, Donald Hall when Jane Kenyon died. It was no wonder their grief expressed itself in poems. But I was not a poet when my near love died. I had written, over preceding decades, a doctoral dissertation, a few articles on medieval literature, the libretto for an opera, a memoir of my mother's reminiscences, all those damned sestinas, and a number of translations. Besides that, maybe ten poems. While he and I were together, I wrote no poems, only funny verses for his birthdays. I'd pretty much laid aside that secret desire.

But a few weeks after the moment of radical separation, writing poems became, not a possibility but a necessity. Here's what it felt like.

> A stream flows from our farewell,
> lands here, has nowhere else to spill
> and in the puddle lies the poem.

It was largely this conundrum that led me to make far love the theme of this long *razo*. To be sure, when my opportunity to grieve presented itself, it didn't feel like a choice. Bereaved people are conscripted against their will into a vast army. Though there are individuals who choose death, nobody ever chooses grief. It feels too awful. The widowed city is too denuded, too empty, to be livable. *Vidua,* empty.

Yet when an unchosen grief became the occasion for poems—poems I had wanted all my life and not found—things got complicated. I wrote, in "The Peter Pan Bus Cycle,"

> I love the poem almost more
> than I loved you.
> If I had to choose
> never to have found the poems,
> and to have you back again,
> I really am not sure what I would do.

Of course I never had to choose, but there have been moments when my own state of mind felt connected to that chapter of the *Vita Nuova* in which Dante vows to stop writing about the living lady in order to devote himself to a beautiful ghost.

This is the place at which I wish to mention that I have had other near loves since the death of the one in the last sonnet.

I still fish for poems in the puddle formed by tears over the absent love, the one that is missing. I thank the near loves for not complaining when I write about the far one. They know that there are still poems to be written about the lost *amor de lonh*. They know enough not to demand that I leave the puddle and devote all thought and feeling to a love nearby.

Just Like the Elephant

Richard de Barbezieux, according to his *vida*, was fond of writing songs containing novel comparisons to animals and birds. We also hear that he was in love, though all we find out about his lady is that she was the daughter of Jaufre Rudel (the poet who dies on the first page of this book) and was married to another Jaufre, Lord of Taunay. The following *razo* tells a tale of their love. Though written in simple language (much simpler than that of Richard's poems), it is quite hard to translate because the ladies in it have no names, and because there are so many clauses strung together with "and."

You have heard about Richard de Barbesieux, who he was, and how he fell in love with the wife of Lord Jaufre of Taunay. She was beautiful, noble, and youthful. He loved her beyond measure and called her Better-Than-Lady, and she loved him in a courtly fashion. Richard pleaded with her to give him the pleasure of her love and begged for her mercy. The lady responded that she would grant him as much pleasure as she honorably could, and, if Richard loved her as much as he claimed to, he shouldn't wish her to say or do more than she was saying or doing.

As their love affair proceeded, a lady of the region, proprietress of a rich castle, sent for Richard, who came to see her. The lady began telling him how amazed she was at what he was doing—how he had long loved a lady who'd never granted him the pleasure of her love—and she said he was such a worthy man, all noble ladies ought to grant him that pleasure and, if he wished to separate from his lady, she herself would grant him the pleasure he asked. She added that she was more beautiful and noble than the lady with whom he was in love.

Thus Richard, hearing the fine promises she made, told her he would leave his own lady. She then demanded he go take leave of her right away, saying she would grant him no pleasure until she knew he had separated from the other lady.

And Richard went away, came to the lady he was in love with, and told her how he had loved her above all other ladies in the world, even more than himself, and now because she had never given him any pleasure in love he wanted to leave her. This saddened and dismayed her and she began to plead with Richard not to leave, saying that, though she had not given him pleasure before, she would like to do it now. Richard answered that he wished to leave her as soon as possible, and left.

Afterward, he went to the lady who'd told him to leave and said he had done what she commanded. He now begged her mercy, and asked her to fulfill her promise. The lady answered that he was not a man to whom any lady should grant her favors; he was the falsest man in the world to leave a lady as beautiful, gay, and loving as his, no matter what any other lady had asked him to do. What's more, she said, if he had left that one, he would leave another. When Richard heard her words, he was more sorrowful than he had ever been in his life. And he went away, and tried to throw himself on the mercy of the lady he'd left, but she didn't want him back. So he, from the sadness of all this, went to the forest, had a house built, and lived in it as a recluse, saying he would not come out until his lady took pity on him, which is why he said in one of his songs:

> Better-than-Lady, whom I left two years ago ...

And when the noble ladies and knights of the region saw Richard's terrible fate, they came to his place of seclusion and told him he should come out. And ladies and knights went to his lady and pleaded with her to pardon him. The lady answered that she would not do so until a hundred ladies and a hundred knights, all of them lovers, presented themselves to her on their knees, with prayerful hands, to beg her mercy, and then she would pardon him if he wished. The news reached Richard, which is why he wrote the song *Atressi com l'olifant ...* (Just like the elephant ...).

> Just like the elephant
> Who, when he falls, cannot get up
> Until his fellows rouse him
> With their bellowing voices,
> I will follow suit.
> My misdeeds weigh on me so
> That if the whole court of Puy in all its glory
> Won't rescue me, I'll never be the same.
> I hope they'll beg mercy
> From the lady who counts
> My prayers and reasonings as nothing ...

This elephant business is not so silly. According to the bestiary authorities, elephants have no knees. When they sleep they must lean against a tree, because if they lie down, they can't get up unless all their friends come and help them.

And right now it would take many elephants to lift me up. A while ago, I was happily writing a book … *Oh, Better-Than-Book that I left two months ago.* I was full of love for it, vowing on the way home from the MacDowell Colony to serve it faithfully until it was finished. Then came Thanksgiving, bringing Owen with his wife and two fascinating teenage stepchildren. Then Christmas came, and Malcolm with his terrible back trouble, and Eulalia and Nellie insisting that he and Grandma Sarah take them to the Met Museum. After all those people had gone home, I wrote a couple of poems unrelated to the book, and then went to Pennsylvania, where something I had written twenty years ago was staged, with music. Then I was full of shame at having let myself be seduced away from my memoir of far love. The things that seduced me are over now, and I could get back to work, but because I abandoned the book, it has abandoned me. I can't find it or hear it telling me how to finish it and make it whole.

According to Pliny the Elder (*Natural History*, Book I):

> in Africk they catch Elephants in great ditches which they make for that purpose: into which, if one of them chances to wander astray from his fellows, all the rest immediately come to succor him; they heap together a lot of boughs, they roll down blocks and stones, and whatsoever may serve to raise a bank, and with all that ever they can doe, labour to plucke him out.

We hear no more from Richard about his elephant. He abandons it and goes on to sing about two other animals and a bird.

> And I am not at all like the bear,
> Who, if he's beaten is still esteemed, and pardoned.
> He recovers, fattens, returns ...
>
> And if I could imitate
> The phoenix ...
> Who burns, then comes out whole,
> I would set myself on fire. I'm so ashamed
> Of my false, treacherous words ...
>
> Better-Than-Lady, whom I left two years ago,
> I must return to you weeping and in pain
> Like the stag who when he has run his course
> Comes back to die when he hears the hunters' cry ...

According to the *razo*—how likely is this?—when the ladies and knights heard that Richard could receive his lady's mercy if a hundred ladies and a hundred knights, all lovers, went to plead with her, that quantity of ladies and knights perforce assembled and went to see her. On their knees (they had knees!), they asked her mercy, and she pardoned him.

 Come Better-than-Elephants! Come Hunters. Pity your prey.

Dante's elephant was Virgil, the guide who finds him fallen at the foot of a mountain and leads him out of the forest, telling him that if he wants to go up, he has to go further down.

> *A te convien tenere altro viaggio*
> *… se vuoi campare d'esto loco selvaggio*

IV
INFERNAL CHAPTERS

Lessons from Famous Sinners

My mother never said "Hell" when she swore. In extremis, she said "Damn," and then apologized. Nor would she read about Hell, which was strange because she was an ardent Dante fan.

While I was studying in Cambridge, she visited my *Commedia* class. Impressed and moved by my professor, the charismatic Singleton, she bought several *Divine Comedy* translations. When his edition and prose translation became available, she purchased all six volumes. She organized a weekly reading group in her upstate New York village. A handful of retired teachers, clergypersons, and friends came together and studied the various English versions. During the long winters, they had time to trek more than once up the mountain of Purgatory, ascend through Paradise, and return to the foot of the mountain, always bypassing the Inferno. That seemed to me like listening to a Beethoven symphony and skipping the first movement.

When I expressed my amazement, Martha replied that the first canticle was too "horrid." She said the whole group agreed. How did they know it was horrid if they hadn't read it? Perhaps they had, in some secret moment, or perhaps had come to their conclusions after leafing through Doré's gloomy etchings. In either case, they chose not to discuss the dark forests, bleeding trees, and excremental rivers, not to mention the final descent down Satan's side past his frothy asshole. They also chose not to meet Francesca da Rimini.

Francesca!

So much has been written about her. Her Tuscan speech, her refined style, her love-death story and its effect on pilgrim Dante—all have been exhaustively analyzed. There's nothing new to say about *Inferno V*, but rereading it in the context of Lives and Reasons, I discover a *razo*-in-reverse.

Razos have a simple way of connecting poetry with love. Jaufre Rudel composes *Lanquan li jorn* because he can't lie in the arms of his *amor de lonh*. Bernart de Ventadour composes *Quan vei la lauzeta mover* because he sees the Duchess of Normandy make love to a rival, Ray. Gaucelm Laudet sings "Ravel and Unravel" because he's in prison, deprived of Lady L. The *razo* describes a crude, perhaps cruel, sublimation that moves from lust to literature, from embodied desire to desire in song.

Francesca's story moves the other way. Asked to tell Dante how she and her lover happened to commit the sin that landed them in their Hellish predicament, she gives the cause, *la radice*, of the deed. One day, she and Paolo, her husband's brother, were reading a French romance about Lancelot and his adulterous love for Guinevere. Several times, the delight of the book seeped into their bloodstream, making them blush. Then, they came to a passage

> when the smiling lips, so much desired,
> were kissed by such a lover,
> then he from whom I'll never be divided
> kissed my mouth, all trembling.

Because of that kiss, Francesca and Paolo, her husband's brother, will forever be twinned in Hell's windstorm. She blames "the book and the one who wrote it" for their plight. She's wrong. Like the unredeemed sinner she is, she's making excuses. Francesca is punished, not for reading, but for a weak-willed lapse from a textual kiss into a real kiss, from poetic lust into lust-in-action.

Commentators sense that Dante feels personally implicated by Francesca's story. What has he, a love poet, been doing all these years if not trying to stir his readers' passions? And how have other love poets affected him? When aroused by reading Ovid or the troubadours, has he only made poems, and never made love? And will future readers of this passage in *Inferno V* never blush, lay aside the poem, and let themselves be overcome by its eroticism? Dante leaves these questions unasked, simply reporting that Francesca's words cause him to fall into a faint. I can still hear the hard c's click and the double d's thud as Professor Singleton spoke the canto's final line: *Cad-di come corpo morte cade,* "I fell the way a dead body falls."

BERTRAN DE BORN

The Hell that Martha and her friends wouldn't discuss comprises nine circles of decreasing size and increasing horror. The place where souls will reside forever depends on the specific gravity of each sin. The heavier the sin, the farther they fall, and Francesca doesn't fall very far—only as deep as the Second Circle. The husband who murdered her has been assigned to the bottom of the infernal cone, not for killing her but for killing her lover, his own brother. That betrayal of family ties lands him in Caina, the icy lake of fratricides.

Just a little higher than Caina, in the ninth trench (*bolgia*) of the Eighth Circle, Dante finds the Schismatics, sowers of dissension. They are in pieces, their bodies hacked apart by demons, reassembled, then rehacked, always incurring the same wounds. Dante finds, for example, Mohammed, *sundered from the chin to the place one farts. The pitiful sack that makes shit from food* hangs horridly between his legs—punishment for butchering so many Christians and dividing the known world in two halves, two warring faiths.

Near the cloven Prophet, Dante meets the troubadour Bertran de Born, who holds his severed head by the hair and swings it like a lantern, condemned because of what anonymous *vida* authors have said about him:

> He exercised as much power as he wanted over Henry of England and his son. But he always wanted there to be war between the father and the sons, and between the brothers ... And if there was peace or a truce, he would struggle to break the peace with his *sirventès* [satirical poems], showing that the peace dishonored them. He reaped much good and ill from this meddling, and wrote many good *sirventès*, of which good things have been written, as you can see and hear. ...
>
> He had a habit of stirring up fights between barons. And he provoked a fight between the English father and son until the Young King was killed by an arrow in Bertran de Born's castle.

The *vidas* also report that Bertran became a Cistercian monk at the end of his life, but the apparent conversion did not convince Dante, who chose this troubadour to illustrate the precise mechanism of divine punishment:

> "I made rivals of a father and a son.
>
> . . .
>
> Because I split persons so bonded
> I bear, alas, my own head
> split from its source in this torso.
> Thus I exemplify the contrapasso."

What I know of fathers and sons I learned when I was married to a handsome classical archaeologist. He and I didn't love each other very well. We only loved the two little boys we brought about. When the boys were still young, he found a woman who did love him well, and he desired to start a new life with her. When, after great turmoil, he arranged to do that, I was so angry and envious that I did nothing to help him remain close to our sons. I thought he didn't deserve them, and perhaps he didn't, but my children deserved a father. I saw them hurt and scarred by the separation, and I agree that dividing fathers from sons is a capital crime, one I've committed, and if I don't acknowledge it, I might have to spend eternity as an amputee in the Eighth Circle.

The Schism

My child, at five,
severed
from his father,
widened his eyes,
fisted a hand,
and said *I'm not ever
getting married!*

Manly words
to conjure
a future emptied
of us, filled
with children
he would not
bring about.

Boys and Wars

Before cutting off Bertran's head and putting him in Hell, Dante praised the troubadour, citing him as a knight of great liberality and as the finest of all war poets, the one who wrote:

> I love Spring, cheerful season
> that brings out leaves and flowers
> and I love to hear the voice
> of birds whose song
> resounds through the woods …

Having heard Jaufre Rudel and Arnaut Daniel sing of Spring, we think we know what's coming, but Bertran's spring fever has different symptoms:

> … and I love it when tents and pavilions
> appear in the meadows.
> I feel deep content
> when I see knights and horses
> lined up in the fields.
>
> I love to see runners
> scatter people and belongings
> and soldiers
> in hot pursuit.
> To see a strong castle besieged
> does my heart good …
>
> And I love to see an armed lord
> first to attack
> on horseback, fearless—
> that's how he fills
> his men with courage.

And when the mêlée begins
each man must willingly
follow him in
for no one's admired until
he has given and taken many blows.

Clubs and swords, colorful helmets,
shields run through and broken ...

and vassals all striking together.
Horses of dead and wounded men
wander around confused.
When he enters the fight
each well-born knight
thinks only of hacking at heads and arms—
any dead man's worth more than a live loser.

And I tell you no food, drink
or sleep tastes as good to me
as hearing the cry "Let's go get 'em!"
all around, and the crash
of riderless horses through branches,
and the screams "Help! Help!"
and seeing men, rich and poor,
fall in grassy ditches
their dead sides pierced
with broken lances, and banners flapping.

...

Lords, pawn your castles,
towns, and cities
rather than give up war.

> Papiol, in good cheer
> go to Lord-Yes-and-No [Richard the Lion-Hearted].
> Tell him peace has gone on too long.

In many songs, Bertran calls on Papiol, his minstrel (*jongleur*), to carry the song to an appropriate listener. At times, it was Lady Better-Than-Good, but more often some powerful prince who might assist Bertran in wresting Altaforte castle from his grasping brother.

. . .

> Papiol, repeat my song
> in the court of my wicked Fair Lord.

. . .

> take my song
> to my lady.
> For love of Sir Aymar
> I leave fighting aside.

. . .

> Papiol, get going
> straight to the Young King—
> say he sleeps too much and I don't like it.

Papiol became a figure in modern poetry because Ezra Pound liked the sound of his name. The young Pound went walking through the South of France, visiting Altaforte and other sites, probing his notion that troubadour desire had more to do with castles and the quest for land than with ladies and the quest for love. Speaking in Bertran's voice, he fashioned a warlike sestina.

> Damn it all! all this our South stinks peace.
> You whoreson dog, Papiols, come! Let's to music!
> I have no life save when the swords clash.
> But ah! when I see the standards, gold, vair, purple opposing
> And the broad fields beneath them turn crimson,
> Then howl I my heart nigh mad with rejoicing.

Ezra-Bertran changes cheerful Spring to a fiercer season.

> In hot summer have I great rejoicing
> When the tempests kill the earth's foul peace …

Every time the word "peace" occurs, it is negated or debased:

> Better one hour's stour [battle] than a year's peace.

> I see [the sun] so scorn and defy peace.

> The man who fears war …
> … is fit only to rot in womanish peace.

> May God damn for ever all who cry "Peace!"

> Hell blot black for always the thought "Peace"!

Thus did Pound celebrate the muscular music of a favorite troubadour and banish Swinburnian sweetness from the realm of modern poetry. This was 1910, and as things turned out, Pound's Europe would never be over-burdened with womanish peace.

> … Died some, *pro patria,*

non "dulce" non "et decor" …
walked eye-deep in hell

. . .

Daring as never before, wastage as never before.
Young blood and high blood,
fair cheeks and fine bodies …

. . .

laughter out of dead bellies.

There died a myriad,
and of the best, among them,
for an old bitch gone in the teeth,
For a botched civilization …

These lines from "Hugh Selwyn Mauberley" are rightly cited instead of the Altaforte sestina in *The Oxford Book of War Poetry*.

Closest to me among war poems is this penciled letter announcing the death of my mother's cousin, here translated into English:

to Madame Gorostaya
3, rue Vauban
Bayonne
Basses-Pyrénées

27 June 1940

Madame

I apologize for asking you to perform a painful mission, that is, if you can do so. I had a Sergeant in my platoon, Frederick Willems, whose parents live in the Landes, in St. Martin de Seignanx. He was killed by a bullet through the eye (instantly and painlessly). I myself am a prisoner and unable to inform his family otherwise than by letter (which I cannot do). Having found in his wallet an invitation to a surprise party coming from you, I thought you might be able to tell either his family or some family friends that you could find in the area, if you don't know Willems's family well enough.

I would ask you, if you can, to get in touch with my family at 13 rue Castega in Bordeaux, because I cannot at the moment give them an address.

Thanking you, and asking your pardon, I beg you to accept my respectful greetings.

E Bougault

Lieutenant Bougault
Prisonnier de Guerre

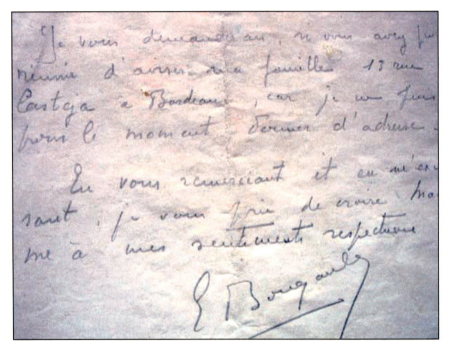

† † † †

... men rich and poor
fall in grassy ditches ...

Young blood and high blood,
fair cheeks and fine bodies ...

Far from the battlefield, yet hardly at peace, my mother visited a Hell of her own from time to time by rereading the letter. It lay long in her desk and now lies in mine, growing paler each time I expose it to daylight.

> A Cousin—how much of a reason—
> lay through the War—through the eye
> the bullet looming larger even
> than Father—even than one
> who—in such cold—made sons
> and went his way—though that
> was later after the harm had been done
> otherwise began—as Mother told—in 1910
> with near approach and shrinkage
> from the Sun before retreat to cold—
> or else those bodies—as was feared—
> without her knowing it—collided
> tearing Planet from Comet.

Paradiso IX

Speaking of outer space, I should mention Folquet de Marseilles, the troubadour Dante meets in Paradise. If we didn't know how the *Commedia* works, we might think he is placed higher than Bertran or Arnaut Daniel because he was a better poet. But you don't get to Heaven for being a good poet. Bertran de Born was a wonderful poet, and he'll never get to Heaven. Arnaut, *il miglior fabbro* himself, is probably in Paradise by now, but first he had to spend a hundred years or so in the refining fire. As for Folquet, he's in the Heaven of Venus, having sung about love, but the reason he's in Paradise at all is that he gave up poetry and became a Bishop.

According to his *vida*:

> He composed well and his appearance was very attractive. He was in love with the wife of his lord, Sir Baral. He courted her and wrote songs about her but neither his prayers nor his songs ever received any pity or any love favors from her, for which reason he always complained about love in his songs. And it happened that the lady died, and Sir Barals, her husband and his lord who did him so much honor, and good King Richard, and good Count Raymond of Toulouse, and King Alfonso of Aragon. Then he, out of sadness for his lady and all these lords, abandoned the world and joined the order of Cîteaux, along with his wife and two sons. He became Abbot of a rich abbey in Provence, which is called Torondet. Then he was made Bishop of Toulouse, and there he died.

It is Bishop Folquet that Dante hears castigating Pope Boniface for having corrupted Florence and neglected his papal duty to launch holy wars. Folquet is described by Pierre Bec, eminent modern Occitanist, as a dry, scholarly logician with nothing of the poet about him. Bec, poet and Occitan patriot, writes:

> Let us add that Folquet de Marseille, during the Albigensian Crusade, grimly distinguished himself for cruelty to the Occitanian population: he was accused by the Count of Foix of killing more than 500 people.

So end my Infernal Chapters and the Lessons I've learned from major Sinners.

V
WOMEN TROUBADOURS

The Paper Creature

In the small college French department where I spent twenty-three years, I often taught the first semester of a course called French Civilization. It was a survey for majors, most of them women, and I regretted that France's Middle Ages, Renaissance, seventeenth century, and Enlightenment offered so few significant females to study—only a few regent mothers of underage kings. French laws of succession precluded full-fledged queens. More importantly, among canonical writers—La Fontaine, Molière, Voltaire, and the rest—I knew of only one exemplary woman poet. Every year I proudly trotted her out.

She was Louise Labe of Lyon, called "La Belle Cordière," because her father and husband were ropemakers. Her written corpus was small—three elegies, one prose debate, and a cycle of twenty-four love sonnets. But a few lines of her sonnets suffice to demonstrate her mastery of echo and rhyme ("*Clere Venus qui erre par les cieux ...*") and her facility with the burning, freezing, wounding, soothing rhetoric of Petrarchan lyric. I invited students to admire her confident claim to the powerful and piteous role of woman/lover/poet.

> We know that every animate being dies
> When subtle soul is parted from the body
> I am the body, you the better part.
> Where are you then, beloved soul?
> [Sonnet VI]

and

> If ever, during my mortal stay,

> I feel my eyes go dry, my voice
> Break, my hand become infirm
> And my mind lose its capacity
> To speak as woman and as lover,
> I will ask Death to dim my clearest day.
> [Sonnet XIII]

The text I presented to the class with greatest satisfaction was a dedicatory preface addressed to a wealthy young bourgeoise of Lyon. In its opening flourish, Louise declares that "the severe laws of men" no longer prevent women from being educated. They should therefore, if they have the leisure, adorn themselves with letters, languages, music—ornaments less alienable than rich gowns, fine jewels, and gold chains. They should aspire to create more than mere needlework. They should prepare themselves to be companions of men not only in domestic matters but also in commercial and civic affairs. They should not try to surpass their husbands, only to challenge them, because up to now, men's superiority had come to them too easily, without their having to strive for it. I assured my students that this was brilliant feminist strategy in a woman of her time. I was always delighted when the day came to show the class her moving words.

But were I still responsible for the Civilization course, that day would no longer bring unmixed pleasure. In fact, I might have to omit Louise from the syllabus and substitute one of her male contemporaries—Ronsard, Du Bellay, or the abstruse Maurice Scève. If I persisted in presenting the Beautiful Ropemaker, conscience would have compelled me to cite a current book, *Louise Labé: Une Créature de papier*, by Mireille Huchon (Droz, 2006). This *seiziémiste* argues that while a certain Louise Labé did live in Lyon in the 1550s, she may never have written a line. According to Huchon, Labé's sparse, strong, and oh-so-feminine writings may have been penned by a group of male poets including one once thought to be the lover she laments in her sonnets. It seems that a coterie of famous men may have perpetrated the hoax, composing lines in a woman's voice and ascribing them to a lady known in Lyon and beyond as a courtesan whose "whorish" mores had been castigated by John Calvin himself from a pulpit in Geneva. Huchon does not offer a clear motive for the prank. Was it pure literary playfulness? Was it a means of expressing or masking the men's own femininity? Was their attitude to women admiring, envious, contemptuous, cynical?

Huchon's hypothesis has received praise and blame from fellow specialists, all of whom have found it, at the least, learned and cogently argued. My amateur's grasp of the scholarly issues does not qualify me to refute or confirm her view. I could easily just ignore the thorny questions and continue to present Louise in her hallowed role as a great French woman poet. But recently, the issue arose in a dream in which I proved a model of scholarly skepticism.

> *I find myself attending a reunion banquet at the college. Around me, emeritus colleagues exchange fond classroom memories with their former students while I sit brooding over my lack of such memories and wondering why I didn't insist on being seated next to my former students—five girl majors and one boy minor clustered at the far end of the table. I try in vain to recall their names.*
>
> *After stewing for a while, I speak up, addressing my far-off alumni so loudly that everyone has to cease their reminiscing and listen: "Tell me, did I teach you about Louise Labé?"*

They pipe up in answer: "Oh yes, the lady from Lyon!" "The noble lady." It is wonderful to hear how much they remember about the dedicatory letter: "Lift your eyes above the spindle!" "The severe laws of men!" Hearing my bright alumni respond, I am overcome with pride. And chagrin. And a perverse glee. "Well, mes amis," I announce, "Louise was no dame d'honneur. She was a call-girl, or "meretrix" as Calvin called her in his diatribe. But we'd be okay with that, wouldn't we? It's fine that she was not a noble poet. But she may not have been a poet at all."

And I proceed to explain the shocking new hypothesis. My dream self, if not my waking self, seems delighted to proclaim the news about "la créature de papier." Instantly the banquet table vanishes and I am in the cloakroom with the tallest and brightest of my majors. She and I embrace in a flood of affection. I feel not a shred of regret at having exposed a great woman writer as a sham.

Why not? For one thing, in my years as a professor, it always seemed to me that one of my main functions was to produce paper creatures of a sort, graduates whose place in the world would be assured by transcripts, letters, licenses—flimsy, equivocal documents like those that had affirmed my own professional status. It had been paper exams and compositions that I required from students and paper grades and recommendations they wanted from me in return. Beyond paper, who were we? I had neither known them nor asked them to know me.

It had never occurred to me, for example, to tell them that I, too, aspired to be a poet. I was spending anguished, ecstatic out-of-class hours trying to evolve a means of expression that would allow me to go out in the world and be recognized as a paper creature. True, I would want to be more than that to friends and loved ones, but with most people, I would be glad to be remembered for a few good poems.

Of course, I would prefer that the work be written by no one but myself. Yet I always suspect that the self who writes poems can't be known for certain by me or by anyone else.

BRUCKNER ET AL.

One of the happiest and most companionable academic projects I ever had was working with two friends on translating the women troubadours. Our book, *Songs of the Women Troubadours,* turned out well—especially the paperback edition, with its cheerful red cover and preface by W.S. Merwin, a troubadour enthusiast. Nonetheless, I'm not happy with the way most of the poems came out. The Countess of Día, in English, without rhymes or tunes, is a pale shadow of a poet.

She was deft at making difficult rhymes fit her music. In *A Chantar m'er ...*, the one song of hers whose melody is known, the *-ia* (of *volria, amiia, sia, cortesia*) clings hauntingly to a repeated musical phrase. I could draw it, and write "da-da-da-dum," yet not convey its effect. In our whole group of thirty-six songs, there are only a few lines that seem okay in English:

> Don't think I'll be slow
> to please myself with joy and youth
> just because it may upset you. (Countess of Dîa)

> I should never have the wish to sing
> because the more I sing
> the worse it goes for me in love (Na Castelloza)

> ... I cannot with my verses
> accomplish what I wish. (Clara d'Anduza)

> Would to God the darkness were not ending
> and my lover were not leaving me
> and the watchman saw no day or dawn,
> O God, O God, the dawn. It comes so soon.
> [anonymous]

Yet a poetry book containing a few likeable lines is not to be sneezed at. And I like more than a few of the original poems printed alongside. Even if readers don't know Occitan, they'll probably know some romance language well enough to get an idea of the melopoeia (word-music) that impressed Ezra Pound. That kind of back-and-forth reading was how Pound and many other troubadour fans, including me, acquired their first notion of Old Occitan, which has never been widely taught, even in graduate schools. I feel like something of a fraud to say that I translated the *trobairitz*. I couldn't have done it alone. I relied on colleagues who are working medieval scholars, up-to-date on the specialized literature, well versed in romance philology. Bruckner and Shepard could have completed the project by themselves, but they invited me to join them because they think of me as a poet, and their flattering view made the invitation impossible to resist.

There are thirty-six songs in the book—more or less all the songs attributed to Occitan women. That's compared with twenty-five hundred or so attributed to men. Our Contessa de Día, the best-known *trobairitz*, is represented by only four songs; and the next best known, Na [Lady] Castelloza, by three. The other women in our book are credited with only one song apiece, or even fewer—a fragment, or part of a *tenso*.

Few *trobairitz* poems have *razos*. I have already given the reason for Lombarda's argument with Bernard Arnaut. The *razo* I'd like to read would explain why a *trobairitz* did *not* compose some song she had in her head, or why a song she composed was not preserved, or got attributed to someone else. In the absence of a story like that, I invented one, based on two lines by Na Castelloza.

WOMAN TROUBADOUR
... on mais chan
e pieitz me vai d'amor

The more I sing, the worse
it goes for me in love.
My Friend carried a glove
beside his skin—
silk, feminine, a Lady's.

I stole it. He said:
"You're pardoned
if you'll sing your song."

Joy spilled into a canzone:
how I suffered,
all I'd do to gain
a small reward. God!
May it come soon!

He took it in,
taught the song
to his Juggler, then,

sent him off
to one of those estates
whose Lord is always gone—
hunting, whoring, warring—
and the Juggler rattled the gate.
"Come in. Come to my room,"
the Lady cooed,
and handed him a lute.

The Juggler stood in the luster
of the Lady's mirror. A man may sing
a woman's song by switching
here and there an end-word—'Oh'
for 'Ah." and vice versa.
Listening,
the Lady paled,
pinked, flamed.

Urgently, she sent for the Juggler's
employer (my Friend), who came
and garnered the reward.
Etcetera. The worse it goes
for me in love, the more I sing.

My name is Alamanda,
Bietris, Carenza,
Gormonda, Ysabella.

I won't grow old. In my whole
life, I'll compose three
perfect songs and lose them all.
I'll shrink into a miniature
red swoop—my gown and hood.

My pen, a centimeter.
My eye, a dot, period.

I imagine that on the whole, it was good to be a woman troubadour—to compose and hear one's songs performed, to find a small audience attuned to one's hinting gestures, to flower, then vanish like pale ink on parchment …

Bels dous amics …

Fair, sweet friend, I can truly tell you
I have never been without desire
since I met you and took you as true lover,
nor has it happened that I lacked the wish,
my fair, sweet friend, to see you often,
nor has the season come when I repented,
nor has it happened, if you went off angry,
that I knew joy until you had returned,
nor …

This fragment is by Lady Tibors. "Courtly and learned," says her *vida*, "charming and extremely well informed … she composed these couplets and sent them to her lover."

"The Little Trobairitz" (a School Play)

Scene: window of a castle in Die, department of Drôme, Provence
Time: early thirteenth century

The very young Countess de Dia speaks with her Uncle and Guardian

COUNTESS Uncle, I'm beautiful, of good mind, and good lineage. Will I marry a powerful lord?

UNCLE I'm working on it, Niece—we're deep in negotiations.

COUNTESS With whom, Uncle and Guardian?

UNCLE Lord Guilhem de Poitou.

COUNTESS Guilhem the troubadour? Wonderful! *She begins to sing:*

> *Farai un vers de dreit rien ...*
> I'll make a song from absolutely nothing
> ... composed while sleeping
> and on horseback ...

UNCLE That Guilhem's dead, my dear. The Guilhem I'm talking to is his grandson. Other possibilities are his great-grandson, Guilhem, and his great-nephews, Guilhem and Guilhem. If they don't work out, there's a distant cousin also named ...

COUNTESS I see that Guilhem de Poitou is sure to be my husband. I think I'll call him "Willy Nilly." I wonder if I'll love him. When I'm married, I would like to be in love.

UNCLE You will be, my dear, but not with Guilhem. You'll love another knight—Lord Raimbaut d'Aurenga—whom you'll meet at your wedding feast:

COUNTESS   Raimbaut, the troubadour? (*sings*)

> *Ara resplan la flor inversa ...*
> Now the flower blooms, inverted,
> On rocky ledge, on hilly slope.
> What flower? Snow, ice, frozen
> Rains that burn, torment, and slice ...

UNCLE   Enough! That Raimbaut's too old. Your *amic* will be a young relation of his—fine horseman, I hear—not a bit musical.

COUNTESS   But I am musical. I'll become a troubadour and compose many good songs about him! (*sings*)

> *Sapchatz gran talan n'auria*
> *que.us tengues en luoc del marit ...*
>
> Be sure I'd have a strong desire
> to have you in my husband's place ...

UNCLE   Ho! I see Lord Guillem is marrying a vixen! But you can't become a troubadour, Niece. You have to be a *trobairitz*.

COUNTESS   Can a *trobairitz* strap on a stringed instrument and ride out to other castles to sing?

UNCLE   Certainly not! You can't trot around entertaining at feasts like a common *jongleur*. Not even a troubadour does that if he's well born.

COUNTESS But two troubadours—Arnaut Daniel and Gaucelm Faidit (the fat one)—were here just last month entertaining.

UNCLE That's because they needed the money. You will have enough money.

COUNTESS (*weeps*)

UNCLE *Oy* Niece. Having money is nothing to weep about!

COUNTESS It is if I can't go to courts and feasts.

UNCLE You can go, but you'll arrange for your songs to be performed by a jongleur. That's necessary in order to outwit the gossips.

COUNTESS Then how will people know the songs are mine? How will Raimbaut know they're for him?

UNCLE You can drop hints.

COUNTESS And he'll understand them? What if only the gossips understand them, and Raimbaut isn't even there?

UNCLE Then you'll arrange for a messenger to carry them to his estate and sing them.

COUNTESS How lovely for him! And will he reward me with the devotion I deserve?

UNCLE I hope not, Niece, for if he does you won't compose your best-loved song. (*sings*)

> *A chantar m'er de ço que non volria …*
> I must sing of what I'd rather not …

COUNTESS Oh! That's good. (*sings the rest of the stanza*):

I'm so angry about him whose friend I am
for I love him more than anything;
mercy and courtliness don't avail me
with him, nor does my beauty, or my rank, or my
mind …

Curtain

VI
THE BRIDGE OF SPIDERS

Endings

There are several ways to conclude a *vida*. Here are some examples.

Jaufre Rudel

... And thus he died in the arms of the countess. Afterwards, on that same day, she became a nun because of the grief she felt about him and about his death. And here are written a few of his songs.

Na Castelloza

... And she was a very gay and a very learned lady, and very beautiful. And here are written a few of her songs.

Peire Rogier

... He had great honor in the world as long as he stayed in it, and then he entered the order of Grandmont, and there he died.

Peire de Valeira

... and he composed poems such as were made at the time, of slight worth, about leaves and flowers and songs and birds. His songs had no great value, nor did he.

Arnaut Daniel

... But it was not believed that the lady gave him pleasure in love, which is why he says

> I am Arnaut who gathers the air
> and hunts the hare with an ox
> and swims against the current.

Bernard de Ventadorn

... And what I, Lord Uc de Saint Circ, have written about him was told to me by the Viscount Lord Ebles de Ventadorn, who was the son of the viscountess whom Lord

Bernart loved. And Bernart composed these songs which you will hear and which are written down.

Uc de Saint Circ
... But he knew well how to express in his songs everything which happened to him because of them. But after he took a wife, he never composed songs.

Gui d'Uisel
... Lord Gui was Canon of Brioude and Montferrand, and for a long time he loved Lady Margarita d'Aubusson and the Countess of Montferrant, about whom he composed many good songs. But the papal legate made him swear never to compose songs again. And for this reason he stopped inventing and singing.

This memoir of mine, like the commentaries of Guilhem de la Tor, is growing longer than the poems it pretends to explain. I plan to end it soon. I just need to mention two other short trips to Occitania.

In the winter of 2004, I read about a village named Auvillar in Gascony. It is inscribed on an official list of *les plus beaux villages de la France*, and it is the birthplace of the troubadour Marcabru (with a plaque to prove it). The Virginia Center for the Creative Arts, where I had done a residency, acquired studios for painters and writers in Auvillar's old port. It sounded like a good place to go in Southern France—far enough from the family tomb, close enough to troubadours. I applied to the Auvillar program and got in. For four weeks in July, I would be working in Gascony. Before I left, though, two things happened.

The first was a momentous anniversary—June marked the fourth year since the death of my most recent near-become-far love. Now the time of his absence equaled (in length, at least) the time of his presence in my life. As a way of finding out what that meant, I wrote *The Peter Pan Bus Cycle*, which seemed to conclude a sequence of poems begun in 2000 in response to a traumatic loss. I wrote

> The poem that going away you made
> keeps reappearing on the page,

but I was afraid this crown of sonnets might be the last thing I'd write for a long time. And here I was going to France to write. That made me nervous.

A week before my departure, I met a man who, I thought, might become a new near love, and that made me even more nervous. It was the old love who had given me all those poems. Would a new love cancel my contract with the old one? Would I gain a love only to lose a Reason?

This is what I wrote that July.

Two Poems and a Razo

One summer, a widowed poet traveled to the village of Auvillar hoping the ghost of its troubadour would help her find new songs. On the third day of climbing steep streets and gazing from various *points de vue* at the Garonne, she said to herself:

> Neither Marcabru nor the limpid light of Occitania
> has inspired any verses. Maybe I should return to New
> York where I have a friend who would console me on
> days when I don't find poems.

Musing as she wandered near the *Gendarmerie*, she happened on a marker that gave Auvillar's old Roman name, and when she returned to her lodgings, she composed this Vernacular Song:

> The birds of *Alta Villa*
> no longer sing in Latin.
> High over the Garonne,
> a garrison has fallen,
>
> but charming *Auvillar,*
> in dahlias and hydrangeas,
> steps down to the Garonne,
> to a port
>
> that holds no boats,
> but only Brits and cats.
> Along the proud Garonne,
> commerce has been given
>
> to the autoroutes.
> Waters
> of the green Garonne
> are altered. All things change.
>
> Only my love
> does not, and won't
> Until Garonne
> flows up into the mountains.

The last stanza took the poet by surprise, as if she'd found it floating down the river in a bottle. "Which love do I mean?" she wondered. "The old one or the new? If that's how I feel about the new one, I'd better go home right away! Then again, had I been home, I wouldn't have written this. Maybe I should stay and see what else floats by in the current."

She stayed, and as there wasn't much to do in the evenings, she and her artist chums liked to walk across the river. The busiest night life in Auvillar took place on

The Bridge of Spiders

People used to fish
on the Garonne,
but industry has risen
through the moon-
light into these girders
lit by incandescent lamps.

Thousands of leggy workers
mend and weave their nets
in time for the hunt.
Between the aerialists
and their victims
affinities exist. Webs

and midges mesh,
like fishermen and fish,
continual darts
of light! Arachnids
entertain us, though they don't
mean to. We look through
frail geometries and think
how handsome the fabric,
how homely the spiders,

> the tipsy polygons
> not doilies but death-
> traps set in the night.
> Next day, we find
> the factory abandoned.
> Filaments, uneaten morsels,
> hang in mid-air. Where
> *is* everyone? Where
> are they sleeping it off—
>
> the effort, the feast?

"Not thousands!" said Mary, when she heard the poem. "Millions!"

(The chums were taking another walk over the bridge.)

"And they wouldn't be here," said Steve, "if humans hadn't learned how to build a steel structure and light it with electricity …"

"… attracting bugs that attract spiders," Mary added.

"Where *would* they be?" asked Virginia.

"They wouldn't be anywhere. They only exist—this many, at least—because of us!" was Mary's sobering reply.

Janet changed the subject: "We're all spiders this summer."

"How so?" asked the Poet.

"Didn't you say you were going to stay and see what comes down the River? That's what spiders do. They spin structures from stuff in their guts without knowing which webs will catch anything, or what the catch will be."

"Right," said Mary. "It could be a fat moth. It could be some dry leaf. They can only make the patterns they like, and wait to see what happens."

The Poet alluded to the story of Arachne, overambitious artist who became the first spider. And the chums all thought, "Could that happen to me?"

"Then again," said the Poet, "there's Walt Whitman's Spider. I loved that poem when I was a kid, but never thought I'd be inside it."

"How does it go?"

"The poet sees *A Noiseless, patient spider ... on a little promontory, launching forth filament, filament, filament ...* He sees himself:

> ... in measureless oceans of space,
> Ceaselessly musing, venturing, throwing, seeking the
>   spheres to connect them;
> Till the bridge you will need be form'd, till the ductile
>   anchor hold;
> Till the gossamer thread you fling catch somewhere,
>   O my Soul.

"That's beautiful," someone said, "but none of these spiders are musing."

"No. Neither was the spider in the poem. She was an ordinary arachnid trying to catch food. She noticed a spider on the promontory watching her and didn't know it was the Soul of Walt Whitman."

That was July 2004, just before my return to New York.

More Elephants and Spiders

In May 2005, I found myself in France again, in Toulouse, on the Rue du Taur ("Bull Street"). In 1955, Paul Blackburn, New York poet and troubadour translator, named a poem after this street. My own "Rue du Taur" begins thus:

> I have been here before
> and didn't like it.
> I'm here again.
> What am I looking for
>
> in narrow stores
> that sell crystallized violets
> and pastel candles? …

I was looking for the Centre de ressources occitanes et méridionales (CROM) and its director, François Pic, whom I'd met in Auvillar ten months before. François presides over a cavernous library on the Rue du Taur, a benevolent spider who attracts writers, researchers, musicians, and others into a widening network of Occitanophiles. Thanks to my connection with women troubadours, he had come with his wife to meet me in Auvillar, taken me on an excursion to Romanesque Moissac, treated me to a delicious lunch, and plied me with books of modern Occitan poetry, though I didn't pretend I could read them. By way of thanking him, I'd sent him poems, including the Auvillar songs and *razo*, and he'd forwarded the work to friends who edit *OC*, a Toulouse review devoted to Occitan letters. To my surprise, the poems appeared on its pages. The poems were in English, and I doubted that many people would read them, but François had introduced me with a genuine *vida*, a paragraph of Occitan prose that somewhat altered the course of my life. It was a portrait of a person I wanted to meet:

> *Sarah White … una poeta americana qu'a passada la vida demest los libres en lengas romanicas…*

Through the veil of a half-known language, I saw myself as I might appear to an admirer *de lonh*—not a Countess of Tripoli, but perhaps a Lady Lombarda—"gracious, fair … and learned, who could compose well, and make beautiful, amorous verses," who lived in New York on the banks of a river as storied as rivers on the Map of France.

> *A la fin de son sejorn dins lo vilatge natal de Marcabrun, confessarà: "Garona es devenguda, tal coma l'Hudson, un de mos flumes interiors."*

The Garonne had become, like the Hudson, one of her interior waterways, and she had brought a measure of—good heavens!—"joy" to Occitania

> *… lo gaug de descobrir una … votz singulara que per delà l'ocean nos unís.*

I wished the *vida* could come true. I wrote thanking François and his colleagues for their interest and asking whether any of them might like to collaborate with me on translations of their poetry. If so, I could submit their work to American journals and return the compliment they had paid me in their venerable review. No sooner e-mailed than done. Poets were convoked, and off I went to meet them.

Now, on the Rue du Taur, I feared that the poets would be disappointed (as would I!) not to meet the heroine of François's *vida*, the intrepid poet-translator. She, having spent "a lifetime among books in romance languages," would master another romance language overnight, translate their work, publish it, and win them an audience in far-off New York. As I made my homesick way along the cobblestones, this intrepid poet-translator was nowhere to be seen.

More Vidas

Saint Sernin
Saturninus (Sernin), first bishop of Roman Tolosa [Toulouse], was arrested in 250 A.D. at the Capitolium, or administrative center. When he refused to pay the required homage to Roman deities, his feet were strapped to a maddened bull, who dragged him to his death. (The poor bull was slaughtered, too, in honor of those Roman gods.) A fine basilica rises on the site where Sernin's body was recovered and buried, and the Rue du Taur marks the short path of his martyrdom, from the present-day *Capitole* to the basilica with its *clocher*—a slate spire atop five hexagonal galleries, gracefully stacked in a brick and plaster wedding cake. The street is lined with souvenir shops, cheap eateries, bookstores, a *cinémathèque*, a bar called La Cave Poésie, and a sprawling edifice housing a few Toulouse University programs, and CROM.

> I have been here before
> and didn't like it
> but I'm here again.
> What am I looking for

in narrow stores
that sell crystallized violets
and pastel candles? At one end
of Rue du Taur

rises the basilica, a martyr's
tomb, rose and cream, a "Circuit
of Holy Bodies"
in its ambulatory

conceals a crystal flower
I've sought and missed—
true fragment of my own
body, on Rue du Taur

One of the poets I met at CROM that day was Jean-Pierre Tardif, whose Occitan poems are published under the name Joan-Peire Tardiu.

Joan-Peire Tardiu
Editor of *OC* and teacher of French literature, he was born in 1954 in the hills of Haut-Agenais, northwest of Toulouse. His father's family came from central France, and only French was spoken in his home, but local people spoke the language of Oc. When Jean-Pierre was around 14, he began to write in "the only language close enough and distant enough to let me speak of my relation to the world." He has traveled and learned languages in Europe and Africa, expanding his world beyond the region where he began to write, but when he looks within himself for the larger world, it comes to him in Occitan, "in fragments" and "from distance to distance." The poems he gave me are filled with spaces and disappearances.

    las causas   òm sap pas ont
             amb
 lo vent

          de finir
      al ras del lisadís

            //

 things   no one knows where
      with
 the wind

       that ends
      in a slipping away

Luckily, the collection he gave me includes French translations. In comparing the translated title, *L'Absence de la mer,* with the original *La Mar quand i es pas* (the sea when it isn't there), one begins to grasp differences between the two languages. I'm not at all sure I understand Jean-Pierre's poems, but I think their disappearances reflect threats to the rural French landscape itself, and to the poet's chosen tongue.

France has never been hospitable to minority languages. Over centuries, Paris has sent brutal crusades, royal edicts, harsh schoolmasters, strict bureaucrats, and talky TV programs to insure that Occitan would become, and remain, a minority language. Though this relentless campaign has never silenced the language, those who love it—like advocates of wolves, whales, and manatees—remain ever watchful against attrition, ever mourning their vanished Old Ones. Just after I left Toulouse, Bernard Manciet, *OC*'s editor-in-chief, died at the age of 83. In him Jean-Pierre lost not only a friend and mentor but an encyclopedia of Occitan lore and language. Here is another poem from *La Mar quand i es pas*.

              the wind gnaws   the days
  as centuries
                gnaw the stones
            into darkness
      houses   down to fire-level
        winter gathering
there   water then water   forgotten
      wind falls
           on the roads
the expanse
    in the hard glow of night
            the sharp cold
and the gnawing
              thoughts

As *OC*'s new editor-in-chief, Joan-Peire does not want to be among the last Occitan poets. It's a good thing there is Olivier Lamarque.

Olivier Lamarque
is very young and very tall. He was born in 1974, in Orly, near Paris, where nobody spoke Occitan, except his southern grandfather, who taught him a few words. He himself did not speak it fluently until, at age 20, he purposely learned and adopted it. He told me he hoped I wouldn't ask him why he writes in Occitan. (I promised I wouldn't if he didn't ask me why I proposed to translate poems from a language I didn't know.) He seems to have learned it in order to speak with friends his own age in his grandfather's language.

He seems to relish using a rare, historic tongue, one he and his friends can defend against the march of homogeneity.

Olivier was teaching in a Calandreta, one of several private elementary schools where instruction is bilingual. I visited his sixth-grade class and talked to the kids—in French, of course, though they read me poems they'd written in Occitan. Olivier told me that none of his students' parents speak Occitan, only their grandparents. Next year, the children will go to an all-French *collège*, where they'll lose their second language unless they make a concerted effort to keep it. I'm sure they would if Olivier were there. He is a good teacher, and a good poet. Joan-Peire praises the way his poems "take risks, renew our vision, propose astonishing leaps."

> *Un curiós adissiatz*
>
> *polida musica de maridatge, òme negre,*
> *dos sòmis que s'encontran,*
> *—quicòm deuriá venir vertat—*
> *coma de sagèls bizantins, de passarilhas*
>
> *lo pitre conflat, entre lèrba jauna,*
> *cavi encara per ela*
> *totjorn per ela*

//

Hello and Goodbye

> lovely wedding music, dark man,
> two shadows meet,

>   —something should come true—
> like Byzantine seals, like raisins
>
> with swollen breast, in yellow grasses
>   I still dig for her
>   always for her

When I met Olivier, he hadn't published a book of poems yet, so there were no French translations. While I was in Toulouse, he helped me find literal English equivalents, and after I came home, we worked on my versions by e-mail. His poems aren't mysterious in the same way as Joan-Peire's and don't, as far as I can see, have anything to do with a vanishing language.

Olivier loves Sylvia Plath and Emily Dickinson. His translations of their poems have appeared in *OC,* of which he, too, is an editor. His first book will come out soon, with French translations. It's called *L'amor es un orquèstra blanc que ne somián los gosses* (love is a white orchestra that the dogs dream about).

The blue mask

> The blue mask
> of the great bimbo
> When the shock wore off
> I stood mute

Jaumes/Jacques Privat
is another editor of *OC,* a good friend of Joan-Peire's. He was born in 1953 in Aveyron, near Conques. He's a painter and sculptor, and in his poems, words become materials to be worked with like pigment or modeling clay.

l'ocra del carretal

*trenca al mièccuts
d'a fons las pradasfrom*

prenon sa realitat las pradas

pel desir suau d'èstre dins tu

d'èstre dins tu las pradasto

//

ochre pathway

through the middle

down in the meadows

meadows made real

by their wish to be in you

be in you the meadows

His meadows, stones, and skies have wishes that resemble human ones—to be fed, touched, sheltered from the sun:

*luna dels
jorns esbrenats
dubèrta poma d'amor
entre tu e l'ochava*

//

moon of
crumbled days
love-apple open
between you and hot noon

Of the three poets, Jaumes is the one who most reminds me of a troubadour. There is some Arnaut Daniel in these lines:

torna-me
se te'n vas
e torna
garganta a la nuèch
deliura
e t'agacherai
pel fengisclet
la lausatha slate
nos farà caud
d'una limpada
me farai
clau
e tu
sarralha
acacholats
pauc a cha pauc

//

return to me
if you go away
return
with your breast

open to night
and I'll watch you
through the keyhole
the slate
will warm us
with your slipping in
you'll make me
a key
and you
A lock
both of us
bit by bit hidden

The poets I met on the Rue du Taur greeted me and plied me with their poems. I thought they must be imagining the intrepid, itinerant poet-translator whom I myself had hoped to meet there, the one who would spread the fame of their beloved language in America and help them save it from extinction. I dreaded their disappointment when they found out the truth—that in time, I might translate a mere handful of their songs, and frame these modest *razos* in a short book.

I did promise to study the beloved language, and when, after ten days, I returned to New York, I brought everyone's e-mail address; the Alibert Occitan–French dictionary François had given me; *Los Vèrbs Conjugats* and other teaching materials; reams of poems from Olivier, Jaumes, and Joan-Peire; CDs—children's songs, music by the reggae-rapper "Fabulous Trobadors" and Marseilles's "Massilia Sound System"—and the sunny voices of the Assimil language method:

Diga-me, l'amic, l'occitan qu'es aquò?
L'occitan, es la lenga del mièjorn de la França, la

> *lenga de l'Occitanìa.*
> [*mièjorn*—South]
> *Perqué la parlas?*
> *Perqué es ma lenga ... es bèla e plan celèbra.*
> [*plan*—very]
>
> (Alain Nouvel, *Primeira leiçon, L'Occitan sans peine*, Méthode Assimil)

These recordings contain the only Occitan voices I hear in New York. As months go by, the friends I met on Rue du Taur seem very far off. For a time, we exchanged chatty e-mails—translations, poems, announcements of readings, concerts, new books, and pictures of Alice, Olivier's baby.

Alice, you must be a pretty big girl by now. Sarah says *Adieu* ("A-dyoo"). (Occitan *Adieu* means both Hello and Goodbye.)

> Adieu, Olivier, Jaumes, Joëlle, Joan-Peire, Francès.
> *Pensi a vos—bonas aranhas ...*

Two Poets Lost as in New York I Study Their Language

> Bernard Manciet (1923–2005)
>
> Max Rouquette (1908–2005)

1.
News is posted on the Web:
Bernart Manciet is dead.
I never met him,
haven't read him

yet, but I've read lines
by Max Rouquette
about the spider
who sets his net
in a stream of *clar
de luna* and thinks
the woven web
turns constellations
pale with respect.

Noiseless patient stars
embrace Manciet
tonight. A meteor
ignites the shed
where hens
put eggs in sweet
straw nests.

2.
Teeth fall out—ripe teeth
that won't bud

in the mouth again.
We needed them

to frame sound
and stop the fuel spills.

The moon will send
no tide this month.

Winds
in a vacant web

weep
Roqueta Rouquette

Cançon de l'aranha
Max Rouquette

L'aranha dau calabrun
calabrun e calabruna
cala au vèspre son filat,
pèr prene lo clar de luna
Fa de tela
son estèla
e crèi que ne paliran
las ensenhas dau cèu grand.

E l'aranha dau matin
son jorn n'es entristesit,
quand au luòc de clar de luna,
vèi cambiat son bèl filat
en fin mocador brodat,
onte l'auba, una per una,
culhiguèt, passant lo puòg,
las lagremas de la nuòch.
E l'aranha au calabrun,
calabrun e calabruna,
Tòrna calar son filat
pèr prene lo clar de luna

Spider Song

The spider of dusk—
brother dusk, sister dusk—
sets his net in the evening
to catch the moonlight.
With a web
he makes his star
and thinks it pales
constellations in the great sky.

And the spider of morning
grieves at dawn
to see no moonlight
but his lovely web changed
to an embroidered cloth
from which a rising dawn
collects the tears of night,
one by one.
And the spider at dusk—
brother dusk, sister dusk—
returns and sets his net
to catch the moonlight.

The protagonist of this *vida* thinks of her friends. Perhaps they think of her and wonder if she ever managed to publish some of their poems in a good magazine. (She has not—at least not yet.) If she fell into a pit, they would be too far off to hear her call, or to come and lift her out. They are in France with their near loves. She is in New York with hers. And here are written a few of her songs.

ABOUT THE AUTHOR

SARAH WHITE studied French and Italian at Radcliffe College and the University of Michigan, specializing in medieval language and literature. After teaching French at Franklin & Marshall College for twenty-three years, she moved to New York, where for the past twenty-two years she has been writing and painting. Some of Sarah's drawings appear in this book. Her books of poetry include *The Unknowing Muse* (Dos Madres Press, 2014), *Iridescent Guest* (Deerbrook Editions, 2020), and *Fledgling* (WordTech Communications, 2021), a chapbook of sonnets.

OTHER BOOKS BY SARAH WHITE
PUBLISHED BY DOS MADRES PRESS

THE UNKNOWING MUSE (2014)

SHE IS ALSO INCLUDED IN:
REALMS OF THE MOTHERS:
THE FIRST DECADE OF DOS MADRES PRESS (2016)

FOR THE FULL DOS MADRES PRESS CATALOG:
www.dosmadres.com